THE LORD'S PRAYER
In Times Such as These

THE LORD'S PRAYER
In Times Such as These

FRANK A. THOMAS

CHALICE™
PRESS
ST. LOUIS, MISSOURI

© Copyright 2002 Frank A. Thomas

Cover art: © Lisette Le Bon/SuperStock, Inc.
Cover design: Elizabeth Wright
Interior design: Hui-chu Wang
Art direction: Elizabeth Wright

This book is printed on acid-free, recycled paper.

Visit Chalice Press on the World Wide Web at
www.chalicepress.com

10 9 8 7 6 5 4 3 2 1   02 03 04 05 06 07

Library of Congress Cataloging–in–Publication Data

Thomas, Frank A. (Frank Anthony), 1955-
    The Lord's prayer in times such as these / Frank A. Thomas.
        p. cm.
Includes bibliographical references.
    ISBN 0-8272-2135-5 (alk. paper)
    1. Lord's prayer—Sermons. 2. September 11 Terrorist Attacks, 2001—Sermons. 3. Sermons, American—African American authors. 4. Sermons, American—21st century. I. Title.
    BV230 .T455 2002
    252—dc21
                                              2002009915

Printed in the United States of America

To my parents,
Almetha King Thomas and John Frank Thomas:
Congratulations on "retirement."
You deserve it and so much more.
Thanks for the years and years of sacrifice and love.

Contents

Preface

At the time of this writing, President George W. Bush enjoys unparalleled public and Congressional support for his response to the tragedy of the World Trade Center and Pentagon attacks of September 11, 2001. The campaign, entitled "America Strikes Back" by the American media, engendered a 90 percent approval rating for the President and emboldened him to pursue with an even greater zeal and determination the Bush Doctrine, his ideological plan to root out worldwide "terrorism," and subsequently make preemptive strikes against hostile nations that have biological, chemical, or nuclear weapons, or anyone that threatens our "security." The President is shifting resources and spending tremendous social, spiritual, and economic capital on security, defense, intelligence, and military operations and buildup, for which the public gives overwhelming support. The President's budget proposes 379 billion dollars in defense spending, 40 percent of the total that all nations in the world spend on their militaries, according to some estimates.

Yet the issues raised by the attack and our response call forth many deep and profound questions that demand intense soul-searching. Amid the many conflicted days and nights of praying and thinking since September 11, 2001, I have needed an anchor, something to hold on to, something to guide my prayers and reflections. Amid the turbulent churning deep within my soul, the spiritual discipline of praying the Lord's Prayer has been an anchor, a refuge, and a framework within which to reach and contact God. And when I contact God, resources are made available to help me think and feel with hope. The eleven sermons that fill these pages are the messages of hope and meaning that I found in the days and weeks immediately after 9–11–01. I found that I needed to have "Faith in the End of the Story," that it was possible to have "A Radical Encounter with the Holy," that God could set up "God's Government in the Human Heart," that there was a difference between "Spirituality and Religion," and that God was the "God of the Amen," to name just a few. These sermons were encouragement as I grappled with the tragedy and trauma of the events of 9–11–01 and their aftermath.

But hope is not the only emotion that came from deep within my soul; protest was there as well. In these days protest, for many people, sounds dangerously like a lack of patriotism and support for the President. While I do not minimize the evil and despicable act that was perpetrated against three thousand families in particular, and the American and world family in general, I cannot embrace the patriotism, nationalism, flag-waving, God Bless America, and the home of freedom and democracy ethos that is recently exuded from sea to shining sea. I register protest! I love this nation, and out of this love I register protest. I wrote a reflection of protest to grapple with the protest side of my thinking about 9–11–01. In praying the Lord's Prayer since 9–11–01 I found protest and hope.

Someone will ask, how do you get hope and protest? Aren't those two separate emotions, and how can they both exist in the human heart? There is the sense that many Americans are having their first experience of "terrorism" on American soil. Well, African Americans have lived with terrorism their entire sojourn in this country. When I see the pained and tortured faces of people who have lost loved ones in the World Trade Center or the Pentagon, I sympathize and remember the lynchings, slave killings, and general mistreatment of African American people. In other words, terrorism is familiar territory to African Americans. We have been here before. We already have experience in the post-September 11 environment. Living with terrorism for so long has taught us about hope and protest, humaneness and anger. We have learned to live with both in our bosom. When one does not have the luxury of bombing to assuage one's anger, rage, lust for revenge, and emotions of hatred, one learns to live in hope and protest.

I would like to thank my wife, Joyce, my son, Tony, and daughter, Rachel, for their patience in seeing their dad "in front of the computer screen again." I express my gratitude and thanks to the many members of the Mississippi Boulevard Christian Church of Memphis, Tennessee, who were the soil in which the seeds of these sermons were planted. I thank so many of our mentors: Jeremiah Wright Jr., the late Fredrick G. Sampson III, Henry and Ella Mitchell, Vincent and Rose Harding, the late Edwin H. Friedman, Ed Wheeler, and so many others too numerous to name. I thank Jini Kilgore Ross, who so patiently went through the multiple drafts word by word and line by line. I thank Martha Simmons, my writing partner, for her friendship and commitment to preaching and writing.

In these days of war and rumors of war, where India and Pakistan have one million troops facing each other amassed on their borders in a five-month military buildup, and nuclear tipped missiles are on standby; where loss of life and violence are daily and much too commonplace in Israel and Palestine; and where the United States and al-Qaida are locked in war with no end in sight, may we learn to say in the words of Jesus in Matthew 6:9, "Our Father…"

The Lord's Prayer

A Reflection of Protest

The protest tradition of the African American church has many notable matriarchs and patriarchs, such as Sojourner Truth, Frederick Douglass, Langston Hughes, Fannie Lou Hamer, and Martin Luther King, Jr. Another patriarch that shapes my thinking is the singer, scholar, activist, and actor Paul Robeson. Paul Robeson spoke words that contribute heavily to shaping the prism of my worldview and the perspective through which I view the events of September 11, 2001, and our response. Robeson said:

> *I am a Negro with every drop of my blood*
> *And every stir of my soul.*
> *And in my Negro heart lies buried*
> *the memory of centuries of oppression.*[1]

When I look at the events of September 11, 2001, through my "Negro heart," I feel hope and register protest. The memory of centuries of oppression shapes a unique perspective of hope and protest, humaneness and anger.

Recently, I participated in diversity training with a group of Memphis community leaders. Our facilitator led us into the very uncomfortable and yet potentially healing place of honest raw emotions in regard to race. About halfway through the dialogue, what I wanted to say bubbled up from within. I told the group something to this effect:

1

All of us know the legacy of slavery, oppression, segregation, and racism perpetrated against African Americans in this country. On my better days, this legacy of mistreatment and abuse I have harnessed to make me more humane, more sensitive to the mistreatment of anyone regardless of their race, class, creed, nationality, or sexual persuasion. On my best days I am compassionate and humane, a fierce fighter for the fundamental humanity and equality of all. Having had the humanity denied to our race, I do not want humanity denied to anyone. But on other days that are not my better days, I am mad as hell at the mistreatment and the audacity of white people to play God. On those days, the anger seethes from me like the heat that rises from the sidewalk on a hot summer day.

I bring my heightened-by-oppression humaneness and my righteous indignation to the events of September 11, 2001, and our response. I would like to report to you some of my thinking and feeling as I prayed the Lord's Prayer and experienced September 11, 2001, and the subsequent events. Through the spiritual discipline of prayer, I have found the courage and insight to face the world in times such as these.

"Our Father"

When I pray **"Our Father,"** the "our" speaks to the common humanity of us all. When Osama bin Laden is painted with the broad brush of "the evil one" or the "very epitome of evil," or countries such as Iran, North Korea, and Iraq are labeled as the "axis of evil," we might oversimplify. When we act as if bin Laden is beyond humanity, the worst and the most despicable human being there ever was, right there in competition with Stalin and Hitler, we might be engaging in exaggerated propaganda. When we lament that he has "hijacked Islam," perhaps we as Americans embellish. While the act was vicious and evil, I remember other vicious and evil acts perpetrated by Americans. I remember American Christians singing hymns and offering prayers at the lynchings and burnings and beatings of innocent African Americans. I remember white-sheeted Ku Klux Klansmen burning crosses, the very symbol of Christianity, to intimidate and announce the murder and torture of African Americans, Jews, and Catholics. I remember then that all of us are capable of the evil perpetrated by Osama bin Laden. Maybe if we looked more intimately and more honestly at our own evil, or our own potential for evil, we would cry for justice, but our cries would be muted with the knowledge of our own sin and need for mercy.

"Who art in heaven"

When I pray, "Our Father **who art in heaven**," it raises questions about what is the ultimate right and the ultimate might. The implication is our Father in heaven is above our earthly parents, and heavenly right and might are above earthly might and right. In a world in which America won a war by remote control, precision guided bombs, and the greatest display of military and technological might the world has ever seen, any nation worth its salt would be trying to get as much of this weaponry and technology as possible. In this world where too often who has the biggest bombs and the most technology seems to win, and might makes right, it is not amazing that nations would be trying to get as many weapons as they can.

We must face the fact that our awesome display of military and technological superiority automatically engenders an arms and technology race. Do we expect the nations of the world to simply "trust" that we will use all of our might for defensive or humanitarian purposes? We certainly do not trust that North Korea, Iran, and Iraq, if they have weapons of mass destruction, are going to use them for defensive and humanitarian purposes. Are we any "trustworthier" than the rest of the world? Are we more peace-loving and morally superior to the rest of the world so that we and our friends can be trusted to have these weapons and other nations cannot? It is precisely this lack of trust that creates the securing of arms and technology at any expense. Of course this brings up the fact that America selectively sells the weapons and technology across the world. Martin Luther King, Jr., said America was "the greatest purveyor of violence the world has ever known." He was referring to our ability to sell arms and technology, often selectively. Often the balance of power in the world has depended on whom we have chosen to give arms and technology. America benefits greatly from a world that seems to operate from the premise that military might makes right.

"Hallowed be thy name"

When I pray, "**hallowed be thy name**," I am concerned that we hallow God's name and not our name. Patriotism is the hallowing of our name. Patriotism is the trivializing of God's name, bringing God's name down to the level of the common and the trite standards of our behavior. While the acts of September 11 are unequivocally evil and the perpetrators at a minimum participated in evil, we must look at some of our behaviors and not assume uncritically that God is on our side. Patriotism sounds as if God supports everything that we do. Patriotism sounds as if God blesses our nation, its values and actions, regardless of their moral and spiritual tone and character. Patriotism sounds as if we are all good, true, and moral. Patriotism can be hallowing a name other than God's.

Whether on the lips of freedom fighters, terrorists, presidents, or other lords and princes, often we take God's name in vain. Lee Griffith suggests that though the human proclivity for violence often reaches a feverish pitch, there is still enough respect for human blood that if it is going to be shed, we realize it should be shed for some cause. What better cause than in the name and will of God? Griffith says:

> With varying degrees of sincerity, world leaders on the eve of battle make a show of consulting "spiritual advisors" and of invoking the name of God. It is a practice not lost on the organizations that have been labeled "terrorist," many of which have incorporated God into the very names of their organizations. In nations in which the majority of believers are Christian, the church must bear the responsibility for the ease with which the name of God has been co-opted into the service of carnage. The preaching of many churches has lent greater credibility to an image of a God who intervenes in history through warfare rather than a God who intervenes in history through resurrection, and the renunciation of death.[2]

It might be that divine sanction for violence could be blasphemy in the highest order. It might be that we believe that God cannot accomplish anything without pulling a trigger or firing a missile.

"Thy kingdom come"

When I pray, **"thy kingdom come,"** I want God's government to be established. Too often I have the suspicion that our government functions not as a democracy, but as what Jared Diamond in *Guns, Germs, and Steel* calls "kleptocracy." As I understand him, Diamond concludes that governments at their best provide services impossible to contract on an individual basis. At worst, they are kleptocracies transferring wealth from commoners to upper classes. Diamond states:

> The difference between a kleptocrat and a wise statesman, between a robber baron and public benefactor, is merely one of degree; a matter of just

how large a percentage of the tribute extracted from producers is retained by the elite, and how much the commoners like the public uses to which the redistributed tribute I put. We consider President Mobutu of Zaire a kleptocrat because he keeps too much tribute (the equivalent of billions of dollars) and redistributes too little (no functioning telephone system in Zaire). We consider George Washington a statesman because he spent tax money on widely admired programs and did not enrich himself as president. Nevertheless, George Washington was born into wealth which is more unequally distributed in the United States than in new Guinea villages.[3]

It might be that George Washington did not need to transfer wealth because he already had it. Is it unfair to ask why the airlines industry was given twenty-four billion dollars as a bailout and not one dime for laid off workers? Is it unfair to ask who is going to benefit from the billions and billions of dollars that we are getting ready to spend under the banner of defense? Who are the companies? Is there a bidding process? What are their connections to the rich and the upper classes? Is it too much to demand that at least half of the profits of these companies be committed to public good rather than private pockets? Do I sound like a socialist when I remind you that Dwight D. Eisenhower warned us of the military industrial complex? We are not just spending our dollars, we are spending the genius of our young people, the hopes and dreams of people all over the world for food for their communities, a decent education for their children, and a roof over their heads for their families. We need God's government, God's kingdom to come that is for the common people.

"Thy will be done on earth, as it is in heaven"

I am reminded that when I pray, "**thy will be done on earth, as it is in heaven,**" that in times of crisis, the will of a few is done. Diamond writes about this reality when he says:

Even in democracies today, crucial knowledge is available to only a few individuals, who control the flow of information to the rest of the government and consequently control decision. For instance, in the Cuban Missile Crisis of 1963, information and discussions that determined whether nuclear war would engulf half a billion people were initially confined by President Kennedy to a ten-member executive committee of the National Security Council that he himself appointed; then he limited final decision to a four-member group consisting of himself and three of his cabinet ministers.[4]

While not in the magnitude of nuclear threat, in terms of leadership the war on terrorism is pretty much the same as the Bay of Pigs. As it should be for effective crisis leadership and management, the current administration in Washington confines the most true, reliable, and up-to-date information to a precious few who control the flow of the information to the rest of government, the press, and the public. Because I do not have that information, I am truly in no position to second-guess decisions at the time of their execution and operation. I realize that Congress operates as a check and balance, but for the most part in times of war and threat to national security, the president's will be done. This is how it has to be, but I am afraid of human will being done.

Human will has brought us to the place of war, disease, and famine. Human will has people starving to death each and every day while some nations throw away food. Human will has, for example, people in sub-Saharan Africa dying in the millions from AIDS while those with access to Western medicine seem to be able to get the treatment they need, and all the while pharmaceutical companies debate patents and making the medicine affordable. Human will! But I look forward to the day that God's will be done on earth as it is in heaven. I look forward to God's intentions, plans, and purposes being accomplished. I look forward to earth looking like heaven.

"Give us this day our daily bread"

When I pray, **"give us this day our daily bread,"** I focus on the word *daily* and the tremendous amount of greed that is in American life. How do we deal with possessions and many people having more than they need in this culture? I interviewed Bernice Johnson Reagon of Sweet Honey in the Rock and asked about a song she wrote on greed. She said she had gone to a conference and talked with a Native American who said:

> Why do we have only one way to understand success—by what we have accumulated? We grew up as Native Americans with the giveaway; so at various points in your life when you feel a certain kind of stability and achievement, you mark it by giving everything you have away. And at a certain point, this giveaway is so deep that you give all your blankets away and even somebody who received a blanket from you might have to lend you a blanket so you'll have one that night. I don't understand why there's only one way to have the idea of accomplishment.

In the song, Reagon dealt with possessions and why possessions are so important in this culture. It might be that we are a nation of consumer-addicts, and while previous generations have been asked to sacrifice to support the war effort, we were asked to sacrifice by shopping. Maybe Bush knows that events of the magnitude of September 11, 2001, take us deep on the inside to what is really important. Possessions and things are really not that important in matters of life and death. To avoid this truth, we are encouraged to get out of the house and shop.

"Forgive us our debts, as we forgive our debtors"

When I pray, **"forgive us as we forgive,"** I'm troubled. I told my daughter that I did not agree with the red-white-blue patriotism and nationalism on public display. She asked me why, and I told her that Black people were lynched with flags being draped and the perpetrators singing "God Bless America." I told her, "Each time I see the extreme and patriotic use of the flag, it reminds me of what Langston Hughes said in *Let America Be America Again*":

> *O yes,*
> *I say it plain,*
> *America never was America to me.*[5]

I thought that I was quite eloquent, but she said, "Dad, get over it." Maybe it was that I was stuck in a time warp and a social protest mode that was outdated. Maybe there is a new black identity that does not need the categories of race. Maybe we do not need Black Studies programs, "set-asides," or any nomenclature that sets us as apart and distinct. Maybe it is more about class than it is about race. Maybe I have not forgiven those who sinned against us. Maybe it is possible to forgive but demand that one's experience be respected. Maybe now I can finally name why, however misguided and misinformed, I felt more trust for Clinton than I do for Bush. At least I had the sense that Clinton respected my experience. Maybe that is why over 90 percent of African Americans voted for Clinton; maybe we could move to a new place on issues of race if one's experience could get respected. In the midst of all of my "maybes" and conflicted thoughts and feelings, what is true is if I do not forgive, then I will not be forgiven.

And Langston Hughes did not stop with complaining about America. He says:

> *O yes,*
> *I say it plain,*
> *America never was America to me,*
> *And yet I swear this oath—*
> *America will be!*[6]

There we are as black people always making America be America. Like the Southern Christian Leadership Conference (SCLC), who believed that Blacks were not simply after a seat at a lunch counter or a front seat on a bus. SCLC announced its mission when it put in its charter, "to save the soul of America." Not just complaining, but we have the task to make America be what it ought to be.

"Lead us not into temptation"

When I pray, "**lead us not into temptation,**" I have tepid feelings of fear, as I watch the recent assault upon civil liberties under the guise of "protecting the nation from the terrorists." To some of us, much of the current language sounds identical to language the FBI used to assault the civil liberties and freedom struggles of African Americans. Former FBI Director Herbert Hoover ran COINTELPRO, which in reality was a counterintelligence program against organizations whose politics Hoover did not like. Clarence Page points out:

> COINTELPRO quickly moved beyond surveillance of Communists to disruption of radical groups such as the Black Panthers and moderate groups such as Dr. Martin Luther King, Jr.'s Southern Christian Leadership Conference, all in the name of fighting communism.[7]

Though only a teen, I was in Chicago on December 4, 1969, when the Illinois leaders of the Black Panther Party Fred Hampton and Mark Clark were killed in an after-midnight raid by Chicago police assisted by the FBI. Federal Officials later settled a civil suit filed by the families of Hampton and Clark for $1.85 million.

Maybe I am paranoid, but I agree with Page when he asks, "In the long run, can we ever know when something as abstract as the 'war on terrorism' has ended? Does it ever end? When might we get our old civil liberties back?"[8] Or I agree with Steve Mufson of the *Washington Post* when he writes:

Many Republicans criticized the Clinton Administration for entering peacekeeping operations without having an exit strategy. It's ironic perhaps, that this administration seems to be waging war without any exit strategy other than moving to the next battlefield. The war could become, as in the George Orwell novel *1984*, a permanent state of being. "War is Peace," the Ministry of Truth slogan read in the novel. Or as [Robert] Kaplan has argued war becomes a condition no longer distinctly separate from peace.[9]

"Deliver us from evil"

When I pray, "**deliver us from evil**," I ask questions about the billions and billions of dollars that will be spent to make us "safe." Where does that take us with all the focus on safety? This prayer of Jesus recognizes several painful realities that we must come to terms with that are contained within the lessons of the attack on September 11. First, we ask God to deliver us from evil because human resources are inadequate to deal with evil and all the eventualities, possibilities, and circumstances of evil, however well planned and organized human resources are. This is not to say that we should not prepare security checkpoints, gather intelligence, screen luggage, and do absolutely everything at our human disposal to protect our safety. But we must recognize that our resources cannot prepare for every eventuality. Life has a certain fragility to it. This prayer recognizes a weakness and destructiveness that are a permanent part of the world and that can be defined only as evil, no matter how many billions and billions of dollars we spend to feel safe.

This leads to the second painful reality that we must come to terms with. Jesus prayed, "deliver us from evil" realizing that not everyone will be delivered in this sphere of human existence. Some died in the collapsing structure and debris of the World Trade Center. Some die when people with bombs strapped on them walk into shopping centers and explode themselves and people's hopes and dreams. Some die from state-sponsored terrorism, ethnic cleansing, and genocide. Whole nations of Native American people died as America waged an offensive holy war for this land. Some children are molested, and some people are raped. Some die at the hands of a drive-by shooter. Martin Luther King lay dead in Memphis from an assassin's bullet. All of us will not escape the tentacles and the clutches of evil. It is not possible for all of us to be delivered from the desperate and despicable acts of evil. Life is fragile, and fragility could happen to you. Evil could happen to you.

If we are not careful, these painful realities will lead us to fear the future, and fearing the future, we will try to spend our way to security. This might be the reality when we realize that Bush and Secretary Donald Rumsfeld seek in their budget next year $48 billion for the Pentagon—an amount 150 percent larger than the annual defense budget of France, the second largest spender in NATO. When Jesus prayed "deliver us from evil," he meant that we could not get around the fact that the future is uncertain, and therefore, living becomes an act of faith, not an act of planning; of trust and not an act of control. This does not mean that we should not plan, but we must place our plans in the hands of the One who can deliver us from evil.

"Thine is the kingdom, and the power, and the glory"

When I pray, "**thine is the kingdom, and the power, and the glory,**" I remember that I have read about some of the great kingdoms and cities of the world. The Roman Empire extended for 1,000 years. So great was the Roman control and domination that there was not war for 200 years during the *Pax Romana*. The territory of the Roman Empire included Europe west of the Rhine and south of the Danube, including present-day Romania, Turkey, Armenia, Mesopotamia, the Bible lands in Asia, and Egypt and the entire northern coast of Africa.

The British Empire consisted of the extended territory composed of Great Britain, Northern Ireland, and the lands and peoples under Britain's control. During the period of its greatest extent, the British Empire encompassed the largest area ever governed by one country. It was said that the sun never set on the British Empire, so vast was its area. Its resources were the richest ever to be controlled by one nation.

And now we have the American Empire—not an empire of land, but of military, economic, and technological superiority. It really is amazing that we can win a war by remote control. We can drop bombs on people from 4,000 feet in the air and never expose ourselves to danger. It is truly an amazing display of technological and military might that the world has never seen before. They even have the capacity to have radar on the helmets of our troops that charts the enemy's position, and they can call in the air support and guide the bombs exactly to where the enemy is. It is impressive. This is the genius of the American Empire.

Charles Krauthammer, columnist for the Washington Post Writers Group, recognizes the genius of the American Empire and defines himself as an "unflinching American unilaterlist." Krauthammer says:

> We dominate every field of human endeavor, from fashion to film to finance. We rule the world culturally, economically, diplomatically and militarily as no one has since the Roman Empire.[10]

America is at her zenith. But the American kingdom will pass—all human kingdoms will pass. It might be that Western civilization and America, the crown jewel of Western civilization, might be passing away, and America is running scared. There is only one continuing city. Thine is the kingdom and the power and the glory in the continuing city. The continuing city, the forever city.

"Amen"

Edward Hooper points out in his landmark work *The River: A Journey to the Source of HIV and AIDS*,[11] that pathological liars are rare. Most people are honest if only because that is the easiest way to live with the most self-respect and a minimum of complication. However, for most people there does seem to be a sliding scale—a point at which lying becomes an option. Many will lie when their self-image is threatened or their financial future is at stake or to protect their family or friends. Only a few people have the integrity to tell the truth regardless of the circumstances or the consequences. Most of us have integrity on some form of sliding scale.

Hooper goes on to say that the process of lying is interesting. One starts by swerving around the sharper and more dangerous corners of what is known to be true to arrive at a position that is almost true. This allows one to maintain two parallel versions of the truth—one for the heart, or perhaps the best friend, or for the spouse in the dead of night. And the other, less precise version, for the potential enemy, for the person who asks awkward questions, and for those who might do one harm. Time passes. Recollections become less sharp. The two parallel versions of truth fade in and fade out and intertwine. Finally the process is completed—two apples become three apples; a chimp changes to a giraffe, a zebra to a crocodile; the truth becomes a lie. And as far as one remembers, one was not even there at the time. Sometimes only God knows what the truth is.

I wonder if in our war effort there is currently an assault on truth and we are majoring in parallel versions of the truth, one for our friends and one for our enemies, in the name of national security. The military's proposed and now abandoned Office of Strategic Influence, which wanted to place fake stories in overseas press, is alarming. Military reporters say that they are handcuffed now more than during Desert Storm. Bush, Rumfeld, and Condolleezza Rice shut down the airing of bin Laden's speeches. Hollywood had a meeting with the President right after September 11. And now the Pentagon is teaming up with Jerry Bruckheimer—producer of *Top Gun, Black Hawk Down, Pearl Harbor,* and *Coyote Ugly*—and Bertram Van Munster of *Cops,* to make a TV docudrama about the war on terrorism. The thirteen–episode "reality" series on ABC will profile our troops abroad. Maureen Dowd quotes Dan Rather:

> I'm outraged about the Hollywoodization of the military. Somebody's got to question whether it's a good idea to limit independent reporting on the battlefield and access of journalists to U.S military personnel and then conspire with Hollywood.[12]

I smell propaganda—two apples become three; a chimp changes to a giraffe, a zebra to a crocodile; the truth becomes a lie. And as far as one remembers, one was not even there at the time.

But what if one learned to live in truth and believed that truth was truth and that truth is the same for the friend as for the enemy? What if one did not have two parallel versions, but one truth? This is the essence and the nature of God—the complete truth—the absolute truthfulness of every word that comes from God's mouth. God cannot lie. God cannot evade the truth. God is the God of truth. God is faithful, and God's testimonies and precepts are sure. To every word that proceeds out of the mouth of God you can say Amen. God is the God of Amen. To anything truthful you say about God, you can say Amen. Whenever God's name is mentioned, you can say Amen. Anytime you mention one of God's attributes, you must say Amen. God is the God of truth, and when we say Amen we affirm that truth will win in the end. When we say Amen we take confidence that a lie cannot live forever; truth crushed to the earth will rise again. When we say Amen we affirm what the Bible says, "God cannot be mocked. You shall reap what you sow." When we say Amen we mean what the poet meant: "The wheels of justice grind slowly, but they grind exceedingly fine." When we say Amen we take courage that right defeated is more powerful than evil triumphant. God is greater and stronger and more powerful than evil. God can take care of and redeem all evil.

Notes

[1]Paul Robeson, source untraced.

[2]Lee Griffith, *The War on Terrorism and the Terror of God* (Grand Rapids: Wm. B. Eerdmans, 2002), xii.

[3]Jared Diamond, *Guns, Germs, and Steel: The Fate of Human Societies* (New York: W. W. Norton, 1997), 276.

[4]Ibid., 279.

[5]Langston Hughes, *Let America Be America Again,* in *The Collected Poems of Langston Hughes,* ed. Arnold Rampersad and David Roessel (New York: Knopf Books, 1994), 189.

[6]Ibid.

[7]Clarence Page, "More Questions for Ashcroft," *Memphis Commercial Appeal,* 11 December 2001, B5.

[8]Ibid.

[9]Steven Mufson, "Evildoers in Bush's Worldview," *Memphis Commercial Appeal,* 24 February 2002, B3.

[10]Charles Krauthammer, "Winter Olympics Aren't an 'Axis of Evil,'" *Memphis Commercial Appeal,* 22 February 2002, B5.

[11]Edward Hooper, *The River: A Journey to the Source of HIV and AIDS* (Boston: Back Bay Books, 2000), 795.

[12]Maureen Dowd, "The War on Terror Goes Hollywood," *Memphis Commercial Appeal,* 26 February 2002, Viewpoint Section, B5.

Our Father

"Our Father" (Mt. 6:9)

I remember receiving a very impressive invitation in the mail. It was in the class of those expensive embroidered and embossed invitations that are sent for some "exclusive" weddings; only it was fancier. What separated it from a wedding invitation was the seal on the back—it was the seal of the king. I was shocked to discover that the king invited me to a party at his palace. I, a peasant was invited; I, one of the poor and uneducated class; I, a sinner was invited; I, an outcast, a leper, an AIDS sufferer, a foreigner, a gentile, a homosexual, a woman preacher, a member of the Taliban, and an Arab. I was invited to the king's party. I am not a part of the glamorous crowd. I am not a part of the high-class crowd. I don't live in the high-rent district. I am a sinner. But I received an invitation from the king to come to the king's palace. And because the invitation was from the king, I accepted and sent my R.S.V.P. to acknowledge that I would indeed come.

I came nervously and was met by the official hosts and greeters. I moved through the crowd with great caution, not really feeling as if I belonged until I saw the king. When I saw him, tears streamed down my face in gratitude and thanksgiving that he would include me. I spoke to him, fumbling and stumbling to say thank you, and how much I appreciated the invitation, and how much I didn't deserve to be there. I was not worthy to be there, I told him, "Thank you for seeing fit to include me."

The king told me that I was not to call him King. He told me not to call him Sir, not to call him Lord, and not to call him Master. He was all of those things, but I was to call him Father. He explained to me that he was offering ultimate intimacy to me in having me call him Father. He was offering a one-on-one relationship between the two of us. Father was different than Creator. Father was different than Master. Father was different than Lord. Father was a term of intimacy and one-on-one relationship. I could stretch my hands to him and call him whenever I needed or wanted to. All I had to do was say, "Father," or as Jesus says, "Abba," which means "Daddy." All I had to say was "Father" or "Daddy," and he would make himself available. He said that he had adopted me as a son and as a daughter. He said that I had not received a spirit to fall back into slavery and fear, but a spirit of adoption. He said, "I have adopted you as a son. I have adopted you as a daughter. You are no longer a slave. You are no longer a peasant. You are no longer uneducated. You are no longer an AIDS sufferer. You are no longer poor or disenfranchised. No. You are no longer a sinner. You are not any of that. You are a son and a daughter. I have adopted you and made you one of my own."

While he was telling me that I had been adopted, his servants brought out a fine robe to replace the imitation one that I was wearing. They brought out some fine shoes to replace the bargain basement shoes I had on. They dressed me from top to bottom, and I felt glorious. I felt wonderful. I felt regal. I felt royal. I felt I was one of God's children. Now every ounce of shame and disgrace was gone, and I was free and clean. I was filled with respect and dignity. The servants even put on my finger a mini version of the king's signet ring. I felt regal. I felt wonderful. I felt grateful to be saved and adopted by the king. And I kept saying, "My father. This is my father." I kept being wondrously pleased. I kept saying over and over,

"My father." It felt so good to say, "My father. I have a father. This is my father." It felt so good to know that the king was mine. He was my father. I felt so very special.

After I left the king's presence, wearing my good shoes, my beautiful flowing robes, and my mini-signet ring, I walked around the room and noticed that others had on fine robes and glorious attire as well. I noticed that others had been given some of the same style clothes that I had been given. I surmised that they must have been adopted too. I surmised that they were sons and daughters as well. But as I recognized that, I began to be jealous, because I wanted to be the special one. I wanted to be the one and only one. You are not special if everybody else is special too. To be the special one, somebody has to be unspecial. It is like that in our families: if someone is the favorite in a family, somebody has to be the unfavorite. I wanted to be the favorite one. God was *my* father. I believed that to be special meant that one of us had to be more special than the other one. There was not enough specialness to go around. God had limited quantities of specialness, and if you had some specialness, that meant there was less to go around for me. "My father" meant that I was the special one.

Then I noticed some of my neighbors there. I noticed some people I didn't like that were there. I saw some folk that I had had conflict with in the past, and I wondered how they got there. There were Baptist folks there: how did they get an invitation? How did the Methodist people get an invitation? I saw some Pentecostals. How did they get in? There were some white people there. I was really wondering how some of them got in. There were some black people. How did they get in? There were some African people. How did they sneak in here? There were some Korean folk. How did they get in? There were all these people that I did not know or like, and I wondered how they got in.

And one of them had the nerve to come over to me and talk about how great it was to be there and how kind and gracious and loving was "our" father. *Our* father? What did they mean, "our" father? No, I thought. He is "my" father. I am the special one. I have an intimate and personal relationship with him, and I am his favorite. He is my father, but he is not your father. You are a coon; he is not your father. You are a nigger; he is not your father. You had a divorce; he is not your father. You are a lesbian; he is not your father. You are an Arab; he is not your father. You are a member of the Taliban and al-Qaida; he is not your father. You are a drunkard; he is not your father. You are a Jew; he is not your father. You are a redneck; he is not your father. You are a fag; he is not your father. Like families at the funeral with two sets of children, one set is clear—"He's our daddy, but not yours."

And when I banished people out of the family of God, my sister backed off me. Then tears came down her face, not because any of the names hurt her, for the king had taken the sting out of all the names. (That is what it meant to be adopted.) Her tears were for what was about to happen to me.

Just at that moment, the king came over and asked me to leave the party. The servants escorted me out. They took the robes off me, and I had to give the shoes back and return the clothes. As an act of mercy, they let me keep the ring as a standing invitation to come back if I could ever figure out why I had been put out. My old clothes were put back on me, and I returned to my old home. I was told that I could communicate with the king, but I would have to call him King or Lord or Master or Sir. I could no longer call him Father.

I asked how and why it was that I could be uninvited. The servants answered that there was something the king could not tolerate: arrogance and judgmental pride. The king could not tolerate anybody judging anybody else when, in fact, everybody was invited to the party by grace. I was thrown out because I had lost the sense of wonder and thanksgiving that I had been invited at all.

This story illustrates three critical lessons. First, if you insist on "my" father to the exclusion of everyone else, you will be escorted from the party. If you insist on pointing out the sins of others, or questioning their spirituality; if you label people according to your prejudices, your small worldview, and your small understanding; if you call people by their old names and according to who they used to be and what they used to do even though God has been doing some new things in their lives; if you insist on being special all by yourself as if God does not speak to anybody but you through your divine pipeline, divine revelation, and divine understanding; if you take everything personally; if you attempt to fix other people or force your will or opinion on other people rather than rely on divine outcome; if you do not relax in the presence of God and enjoy the fact that you are saved and sanctified and have been invited to the party, instead of being uptight and looking around to try to figure out how she got there, how he got there, and who's there, then you will be escorted from the party. If you label others as evil without acknowledging your own evil; if you insist on "my" father rather than "our" father, you will be asked to go back home.

Second, prayer is not exclusively an individual exercise. You and I are not in the business of "me and my Lord alone." We cannot retreat into our own worlds and make ourselves individualistic and infallible. God demands that we say "our" to force us to push beyond our own limited perspective. God makes you and me say "our" to push past the people who think like you, feel like you, look like you, worship like you, talk like you, and sing like you. God makes us say "our" because sacred music is larger than spirituals. It's larger than anthems. It's larger than praise music. It's larger than traditional gospel. Larger! God makes us say "our" because the kingdom is bigger than the Disciples of Christ, bigger than the Baptists, bigger than the Methodists, bigger than the nondenominationalists, bigger than the Pentecostals. God makes us say "our" because the children of God are bigger than your ethnicity or your socioeconomic background, bigger than your middle-class neighborhood. God has us say "our" because salvation is bigger than our traditions; truth is bigger than our theologies; and wisdom is deeper than our seminaries. God has us say "our" to push past our boundaries. Jesus never said "my" father; he went and had dinner with sinners and tax collectors and said "our" father. He did not say "my" with the self-righteous scribes and Pharisees, but went to prostitutes and lepers and said "our." God demands that we say "Our Father."

Third, if you received an invitation to the party, it was simply because of the king's generosity. It's not because of your degrees or your good looks; it's not because of your pedigree. It's not how long you have been a member of the church or how many years your family has been involved. It's not because you are a tither. It's not any of that. It has very little to do with you and a whole lot to do with the generosity of the king. If you have been invited, it's because of the king. It is about the mercy, compassion, grace, and loving-kindness of God Almighty, who is our father. It is not about you. You might be able to call God "Lord," or you might be able to call God "Creator." You might be able to call God "Master," and you can call God "Sir" if you please, but to call God "Father," you have to have an invitation.

In other words, when you forget to be grateful or when you remove the focus from your life and the many mistakes you have made and the many times you have fallen down and fallen short...when you take the focus off your self and your shortcomings and how amazing this grace is that has included you, and how amazingly loving and kind God is to have invited you...when you take your eyes off that, you start to snoop around and wonder how she got in and how he got in, and what he's doing and what she's doing. You have taken your eyes off the grace that has been extended to you. And you never want to do that.

You never want to stop saying thank you for my invitation. Thank you for calling me. Thank you for saving me. Thank you for delivering me. Thank you for taking a kid off the south side of Chicago and making him into something. Thank you for allowing me to preach this gospel. Thank you for giving me a wife and a wonderful family. Thank you for what you're doing even right now. I just keep saying thank you.

I'm so busy praising my Jesus, I ain't got time to wonder how you got to the party. I'm so busy telling God thank you, I don't care who you used to go with, what you used to do. I'm not worried about whether you are a lesbian. I don't care if you've made some mistakes. I'm so busy giving God the glory for my getting in the door that I'm just glad to see you. I'm glad to say, "Our Father." I'm glad to share my daddy with you. I'm glad to see you. Bring your praise and add it to my praise. Bring your joy and add it to my joy. Bring your laughter and add it to my laughter. And together, we will give God some praise.

This is my testimony, and I think that it might be yours too:

> *I was sinking deep in sin, far from the peaceful shore,*
> *very deeply stained within, sinking to rise no more.*
> *But the Master of the sea heard my despairing cry,*
> *from the waters lifted me, now safe am I.*
> *Love lifted me. Love lifted me.*
> *When nothing else could help, love lifted me.*[1]

Am I by myself or can you help me when I say, "Oh, when I think of the goodness of Jesus and all he has done for me, my soul cries out 'Hallelujah! Thank God for saving me.'" I thank God for saving you. He is our father. Do you need a father? I am glad to share mine with you. I have a good daddy. I have an awesome daddy. I have a wonderful daddy. I have a powerful daddy. I am so glad to share my father with you. I am so glad to say, "Our Father."

Note

[1]James Rowe, "Love Lifted Me" (1912).

Oh, What a Beautiful City

"Our Father who art in heaven"
(Mt. 6:9)

I walk around with a deep sadness borne of the events of Tuesday, 9–11–01, that is almost a perpetual heaviness. I stare at the television in disbelief. On every station there is breaking news, late-breaking news, clarification of the late-breaking news, correction of the late-breaking news, interviews, pundits, pictures, emergency personnel, video footage, shock and amazement, and the never ending rerunning of the airplanes hitting the towers of the World Trade Center. I am burned-out on the coverage, and yet I cannot stay away from it. I live with the expectation that soon bombs will be falling in our world somewhere, if for no other reason than retribution. War. Why this piercing depression, this grief, this heaviness, this profound sadness? The only relief is prayer: "Our Father who art in heaven." I kept praying over and over again, "Our Father who art in heaven."

In the midst of my prayer, the news media put a microphone under my nose and ask me, "You say there is relief in praying 'Our Father in heaven'; Where is heaven? What is heaven? Is it a place? A condition of life? Is it the opposite of

Adapted from the sermon preached at Mississippi Boulevard Christian Church, Memphis, Tennessee, on the Sunday after September 11, 2001.

hell? Is it far away or close at hand? Is it up there in the sky somewhere, or is it in the human heart? Is it a dream? Do airplanes run into buildings in heaven? And in this time of national tragedy, why do you get such comfort from heaven? Our viewing audience would like to know, exactly what is this heaven that you are referring to?"

Heaven is a vision of home that God places in the hearts of Christians the moment that they acknowledge Jesus as Lord and Savior. Heaven is the place that describes the sun, moon, stars, sky, and numberless galaxies flung across the infinite expanses that are the home of the realm, reign, and rule of God. Heaven is the place that Jesus describes in John 14:2 when he says, "In my Father's house are many rooms…I am going there to prepare a place for you." Heaven is the crystal city, the new Jerusalem, a home especially prepared for God's children (Revelation 21). Heaven is God's dwelling place. Heaven is the realm of God. Heaven is the ultimate place of hope for the Christian.

God has planted the vision of heaven into my bosom, and the greater the tragedy on this planet, the clearer the vision of heaven expands in my imagination. The greater the pain here, the more alive heaven is in my heart. I do not know what could be more devastating than airplanes guided by suicide bombers into crowded buildings. When I see the collapse of the first tower, then the second tower of the World Trade Center, I know that this is an almost unimaginable evil. Lee Griffith speaks to the extraordinary nature of evil in this act when he says; "The skies of New York City were clear and bright on September 11, 2001, when it started raining human beings."[1] When I contemplate the loss of life, and the loss of life that will be in response to this loss of life, then my heart thinks about heaven and says, "Oh, what a beautiful city. Twelve gates to the city, hallelu!"

There are five characteristics of heaven that the Christian holds dear. These characteristics are missing here on earth, or such events as the World Trade Center bombing would not occur.

First, heaven means a satisfaction and contentment that are not known here. The fundamental human condition is that we are not satisfied nor content. There is restlessness in our spirits. Some have said there is a hole in the heart that nothing but God can fill. And because there is a hole in our hearts, we reach outside of ourselves to the world to be full. And because we look to others to fill a void they cannot fill, we are disappointed. Many of us live with an inner ache from the disappointment. We know that we were made to live better and higher, but cannot on this planet attain what we were created to be.

But in heaven, there is no disappointment. Heaven means a satisfaction and contentment that are not known here. God is complete contentment and enduring repose, and no one needs to look for anything in any form of restlessness. God's presence is the full measure of what anyone could ever need. God's presence causes us to live higher, to our full potential. We were made to live in contentment and enduring repose, and therefore heaven is our home.

The symbol for the complete contentment and the enduring repose of heaven is the New Jerusalem that comes down from the sky in Revelation: 21:1–4 says:

> Then I saw a new heaven and a new earth, for the first heaven and the first earth had passed away, and there was no longer any sea. I saw the Holy City, the new Jerusalem, coming down out of heaven from God, prepared as a bride beautifully dressed for her husband. And I heard a loud voice from the throne saying, "Now the dwelling of God is with men, and he will live with them. They will be his people, and God himself will be with them and be their God. He will wipe every tear from their eyes. There will be no more

death or mourning or crying or pain, for the old order
of things has passed away."

Second, heaven means absolute justice and fairness.
Violence is often the response of human beings or human
societies who feel a lack of justice and fair treatment. They
seek address and redress of their concerns through bloodshed.
We watch with horror as someone seeks to redress grievance
by running fuel-laden planes into buildings, killing thousands
of people.

In truth, we must admit that human beings are quick to
exploit each other, and some grievances are legitimate. We
must also admit that we are slow to recognize when we have
treated someone else unfairly. But in heaven there is the God
of absolute fairness and justice who will address and redress
every concern. In heaven, there will be no exploitation of
other people, such as discrimination, unfairness, scheming,
conniving, and fast talk. In heaven we will be quick to
recognize when we have treated someone unfairly, and redress
it immediately. In heaven an all-seeing and all-wise God rules,
who judges all things fairly, and there is no violence.

The absolute fairness and justice of God is symbolized by
God's throne. Revelation 20:11–12 says:

> Then I saw a great white throne and him who was
> seated on it. Earth and sky fled from his presence, and
> there was no place for them. And I saw the dead, great
> and small, standing before the throne, and books were
> opened. Another book was opened, which is the book
> of life. The dead were judged according to what they
> had done as recorded in the books.

Third, heaven means exquisite fellowship. Because we
have not treated everyone fairly, and most of the time we are
slow to recognize when we have been unfair and quick to
recognize when someone has been unfair to us, there are

breaks in relationship and breaks in fellowship. We cannot all sit down at the table together and have food and fellowship; certainly the United States and the Taliban, Palestinians and Israelis, Indians and Pakistanis have a hard time sitting down together and having fellowship. The rich have a hard time sitting down with the poor when some have nothing at all while others have everything. We cannot have fellowship when some throw away food in waste while others have nothing to eat. We cannot have fellowship when some have medicine, food, and clothing and others have nothing. We cannot have fellowship when some live in penthouses and others live in shacks. How can we eat together? How can we all sit at the table and laugh and have fellowship?

In heaven, there is no fractured relationship where some have and others do not have. In heaven everyone has. This happy state is symbolized by the pure water of life that flows from the crystal throne of God. Pure water is a symbol of the exquisite fellowship and relationship in heaven. Revelation 21:6, 22:1 says:

> He said to me: "It is done. I am the Alpha and the Omega, the Beginning and the End. To him who is thirsty I will give to drink without cost from the spring of the water of life"…Then the angel showed me the river of the water of life, as clear as crystal, flowing from the throne of God and of the Lamb down the middle of the great street of the city. On each side of the river stood the tree of life, bearing twelve crops of fruit, yielding its fruit every month. And the leaves of the tree are for the healing of the nations.

Fourth, heaven is the destruction of evil and the place of ultimate and final victory of God. Heaven is the place where we come to see that the battle was not against flesh and blood. We will see that it was not against people and groups of people at all. We will see that there are powers and principalities.

There were rulers of spiritual darkness and spiritual wickedness in high places that moved behind the scene directing things for evil and disaster. We will see how easy it was for our neighbor to be deceived and for us to be deceived. We will see the tricks and manipulations the enemy used to keep the human family apart. We will see that we had more in common than we had apart—that though we focused on the differences, our commonality as creatures of God could have made us one. All of the battles and struggles with Satan will be over, and we will reign with Christ forever.

The symbol of the victory is that fire came down from heaven to save the Christians and defeat Satan once and for all. Revelation 20:7–10 says:

> When the thousand years are over, Satan will be released from his prison and will go out to deceive the nations in the four corners of the earth—Gog and Magog—to gather them for battle. In number they are like the sand on the seashore. They marched across the breadth of the earth and surrounded the camp of God's people, the city he loves. But fire came down from heaven and devoured them. And the devil, who deceived them, was thrown into the lake of burning sulfur, where the beast and the false prophet had been thrown. They will be tormented day and night for ever and ever.

Fifth, heaven is the place of the pure worship of God. Heaven is the place where there is the pure praise of God. The response of heaven to the victory of God is the pure and perfect praise of God. The response of heaven is joy, thanksgiving, worship, and praise.

The symbol of worship, praise, and adoration of God is the word *Hallelujah* which means "praise God." We get a glimpse of the heavenly praise in Revelation 19:4–7:

The twenty-four elders and the four living creatures fell down and worshiped God, who was seated on the throne. And they cried: "Amen, Hallelujah!" Then a voice came from the throne, saying: "Praise our God, all you his servants, you who fear him, both small and great!" Then I heard what sounded like a great multitude, like the roar of rushing waters and like loud peals of thunder, shouting: "Hallelujah! For our Lord God Almighty reigns. Let us rejoice and be glad and give him glory!"

Heaven means these five things to the Christian: complete contentment and enduring repose; absolute fairness and justice; exquisite fellowship; the ultimate and final victory of God; and pure praise, worship, and adoration of God.

In the midst of this tragedy of 9–11–01, I see heaven because I come from a people who have historically seen heaven in tragedy. The Negro spiritual is the creative, imaginative, and celebrative response of the slave to the degradation of slavery, or as John Lovell says, "the free heartbeat of a chained people."[2] To many slaves the image of heaven was metaphor for the reality of a time and place where the slave would be free. Heaven was a city where there would be no slavery, death, disease, sickness, and so forth. In heaven, the slave would be free, in all the implications of what that word means. The slave became overwhelmed in his or her imagination at this possibility of freedom, and expansively exclaimed, "Oh what a beautiful city! Oh, what a beautiful city!" The slave received powerful hope and courage from the heavenly city, the image of the new Jerusalem that came down from heaven and John saw in Revelation 21.

I heard Kathleen Battle and Jessye Norman sing a spiritual about heaven entitled, "Oh, What a Beautiful City."[3] They sang these very simple words:

Oh, what a beautiful city! Oh what a beautiful city!
Oh, what a beautiful city! Twelve gates to the city,
 hallelu!
Three gates in the east; three gates in the west;
Three gates in the north; three gates in the south.
Oh, what a beautiful city!
Twelve gates to the city, hallelu!

When they got through singing, heaven was so vivid and real that I could say as John did, "I saw a new heaven and a new earth...I saw...the new Jerusalem" (Rev. 21:1). When they finished singing, heaven was present, in the room, available. And the tears flowed from deep within my heart at the beauty and the possibility of freedom. Heaven was just that real! All I could say was, "Oh, what a beautiful city." When I looked at the devastation of the World Trade Center, I became overwhelmed in my imagination at the possibility of heaven and said again, "Oh, what a beautiful city."

When I look at the division between America, Afghanistan, Pakistan, Palestine, Israel, Saudi Arabia, and a host of others, I am thankful that there are three gates in the north, three gates in the south, three gates in the west, and three gates in the east. These many gates are needed because everyone is welcome. There are twelve gates in the city to receive people, regardless of race, class, religion, or social status. Oh, what a beautiful city.

I don't know about you, but while I was watching CNN, I was down and crying. Then all of a sudden a breaking news flash came into my soul: "Our Father who art in heaven..." I got a glimpse of heaven, and this good news on a bad day reminded me of heaven:

There is somebody above all of this.
There is a plan beyond all of this.
There is a love that is deeper than all of this.
There is a heaven that is higher than all of this.

Oh, what a beautiful city! Oh what a beautiful city!
Oh, what a beautiful city! Twelve gates to the city,
   hallelu!

Notes

[1]Lee Griffith, *The War on Terrorism and the Terror of God* (Grand Rapids: Wm. B. Eerdmans, 2002), ix.

[2]John Lovell, Jr., *Black Song: The Forge and the Flame* (New York: Paragon House), 1986.

[3]Kathleen Battle and Jessye Norman, *The Spirituals,* recorded live in Carnegie Hall, New York, 18 March 1990, (Hamburg: Deutsche Grammophon, Compact Disc, 1991).

A Radical Encounter with the Holy

"Hallowed be thy name" (Mt. 6:9)

In *The Trivialization of God: The Dangerous Illusion of a Manageable Deity*,[1] author Donald McCullough teaches that the church has lost its sense of awe and mystery pertaining to the holiness of God. McCullough believes that we have whittled God down to a nice and comfortable deity who fits neatly into our precise doctrinal positions; a god who supports our social crusades and outreach ministries, but never stirs up the waters; a god who approves of our casual spiritual experiences and our obligatory and perfunctory worship. McCullough, and I agree with him, suggests that reverence and awe for God have been replaced by the hushed yawn of familiarity and the rigidity of legalistic tradition. We have lost the sense of God as radical encounter with the holy.

As a matter of fact, a committed member of the church said the same thing as McCullough without ever reading McCullough. A committed church member said, "Our sense of worship, awe, and mystery of God have fallen to the level that many people don't know the difference between emotionalism and spirituality." Many of us think that emotion automatically indicates the presence of God, especially the feel-good emotion. As long as we feel good, we know the Holy Spirit is moving and blessing in the service. I want to suggest that the Holy Spirit does more than make you me feel good. Sometimes, the Holy Spirit makes me mad. Sometimes the Holy Spirit gets on my nerves. Sometimes the Holy Spirit convicts me of my sin. Convicts me: I'm not living right. Convicts me: I'm not acting right. Convicts me of my hard heart and my stiff neck, and I don't always feel good when I am confronted and challenged. Because we have lost the true sense of the mystery and the awesomeness of the Almighty God, we have substituted emotionalism for spirituality. We have become "too common" with God.

"Too common." I haven't heard that phrase in a long time. I remember that older people would say to us young folks, especially to the young ladies, "You had better be careful; you're just a little bit too common with him." This was usually stated in reference to the physical closeness and the liberal access to her body that a young woman was allowing a young man who lacked the appropriate wedding credentials. To be common is to grant someone privileges and access that are not appropriate, and to which they are not entitled. To be common is acting as though you are automatically supposed to have access rather than realizing that access is only granted by invitation. To be common, or too common is inviting yourself to take liberties that are not really yours, or allowing someone to take liberties that are not really theirs.

That's what we do with God and God's name. We're too common. We throw it around without respect. Terrorists throwing around God's name—holy wars and jihads—and I heard one of them say, "We're fighting for God." We are too common with God's name. What about pogroms, crusades, the slave trade, and apartheid? Does it bother anybody that much of the justification for these acts of violence was God's name? President Bush and America just throwing around God's name. We have catchy phrases and cute slogans that we do not really mean, like "In God we trust." Just throwing around God's name as if God agrees with everything that we do around the world, as if God does not appropriately have a word of judgment for America, as if God will not critique our behavior. But instead assuming that God is going to automatically bless America is just throwing around God's name.

Too common. In popular culture we just throw around God's name. It is "G-d this" and "G-d that." In many movies and videos and CDs, hardly anything is said without the four-letter words. We have comedians who—if you took out the four-letter words—wouldn't know how to tell a joke. I like Bill Cosby, who can tell a joke without needing to curse to be funny. I like Sinbad, who does not curse in his performances, but still is hilarious. When I was growing up, adults would stop our cursing and say, "Don't use the Lord's name in vain." I believe they were saying, "Don't be too common with God. Hallowed be God's name."

While we are being too common, Jesus says, "Hallowed be thy name." Jesus is making plain that God's name must be made holy, that is, reverenced and respected. While we are taking God's name in vain, Jesus prayed, "Hallowed be thy name." Jesus petitioned God to be God, asked God to break forth in revelation as the Holy One in our midst. Jesus petitioned for radical encounter with God. When Jesus prayed, "Hallowed be thy name," his first concern and deepest passion was that God would be holy upon the earth. Jesus prayed that God would be revealed as holy and revered as holy, not as the manageable deity often portrayed in the average church, but as the holy God who brings purity to the earth.

The word *holy* means that which is set apart, that which is marked off and withdrawn from everyday use, that which is special and not common—sacred. Holy has connotation with the Latin word *integer*, where we get our word *integrity*, which means W-H-O-L-E, having no broken parts, being of full consistency; uncontaminated, pure, no divisions, no fracture, and no alloy. Holiness is a divine wholeness, divine otherness that is worthy of worship and veneration. Holiness comes into our ordinary human reality and transforms it, and whenever holiness comes in contact with the mundane, radical encounter is the result.

Holiness has to do with that which is separate and separated for divine use. First, in the Old Testament, objects are set apart: the burning bush, Jerusalem, the ark of the covenant, the temple, and the place in the temple known as the Holy of Holies. **Holiness has to do with things set apart for God's service.** Second, holy is applied to the name and the person of God, the utter uniqueness of the nature and the person of God. God is holy (1 Pet. 1:16). God is the Holy One of Israel. **Holiness is characteristic of the nature and person of God** Third, holiness embodies an ethical dimension: "Be holy because I, the LORD your God, am holy" (Lev. 19:2). The prophets angrily blast perfunctory worship and call the people to live holy by correcting oppression, defending the fatherless, and pleading for the widow. **Holiness is a code of conduct and ethic for behavior.** God is utterly distinct and set apart in the Old Testament, and we should be holy just as God is holy. But what is there for us when we cannot be holy?

This sets the stage for Jesus, who is the human fulfillment of the essence of God's nature as holiness and God's ethic of holiness. Jesus did not have a radical encounter; he *was* the radical encounter. The Holy One of Israel is revealed in the Holy One of Nazareth. In Jesus, God is separate and holy but available for love and redemption because God knows that we cannot be holy. In Jesus, the world is judged as being not holy, but Jesus takes that judgment and nails it to a cross. Jesus is brought forth from the grave, offering redemption and mercy. In Jesus, God is wholly other—outside of the realm of our understanding and our knowledge, and when we cannot be like God, in the death and resurrection of Jesus the Christ this complete mercy and grace establish our relationship with God. In Jesus, God donned the humble clothing of human flesh that we might don the clothing of holiness.

Isaiah caught a glimpse of the holiness of God and of the human filth in the presence of God that is overcome in Jesus. Isaiah has a radical encounter and says:

> In the year that King Uzziah died I saw the Lord sitting upon a throne, high and lifted up; and his train filled the temple. Above him stood the seraphim; each had six wings: with two he covered his face, and with two he covered his feet, and with two he flew. And one called to another and said: "Holy, holy, holy is the Lord of hosts; the whole earth is full of his glory." And the foundations of the thresholds shook at the voice of him who called, and the house was filled with smoke. And I said: "Woe is me! For I am lost; for I am a man of unclean lips, and I dwell in the midst of a people of unclean lips; for my eyes have seen the King, the Lord of hosts!" (paraphrase of Isa. 6:1–5)

Isaiah knew that he could stand his own uncleanness; however, it was another thing to be in the presence of a God who is pure and holy. In the presence of God, radical encounter begins when we realize that all our excuses must stop and all our lies and deceits must cease. In the presence of this God, you must admit that you are not clean. In the presence of this God, you must acknowledge your sin. Isaiah said, "Woe is me...for I am a man of unclean lips, and I dwell in the midst of a people of unclean lips." Isaiah expected to die. Isaiah knew that this God was a consuming fire. Isaiah knew that this God demanded purity.

Our God is not safe. You cannot appear before the Holy One with steady knees. When you encounter this God, the hair on your head stands on end. In the presence of this God human indifference gets slapped to alert attention, and human pretension gets knocked on its backside. This God is a threat to the status quo. This God cannot be contained in any one denomination, cannot be circumscribed by any one nation or limited by one ethnicity. This God will not stay put in obligatory and perfunctory worship. This God breaks out of the hushed yawn of familiarity and the rigidity of legalistic tradition. This God is not locked into the altar or chained to the communion table or handcuffed to the pulpit. This God does not stay in places assigned to God by human egos desperately trying to maintain control. Hallowed be thy name, for our God is holy. When you come in contact with this holy God, get ready for a radical encounter.

Isaiah discovers that when he expects death, God offers mercy and grace. God appoints an angel to take a hot coal and touch his lips; thus, Isaiah is made clean. The angel says, "This has touched your lips, and you are made clean." So Isaiah discovers that the purpose of holiness is not just for judgment but for cleansing. Isaiah discovers the purpose of holiness is not just to point out faults but also to make him whole. After God cleans him up, God offers him a mission: "Whom shall I send, and who will go for us?" (6:8)

Radical encounter always leads to divine mission. Radical encounter reveals divine purpose, and divine purpose offers a divine invitation, and divine invitation offers divine mission. Isaiah takes up the divine mission. Isaiah responds to the question and says, "Here am I. Send me." Isaiah has been made holy.

As I go to my seat, I want to say, Hallowed be thy name. Hallowed be thy name. Holy, holy, holy Lord God of hosts. Heaven and earth are full of your glory. Hallowed be thy name. God, give us a radical encounter! God, give us a deepened sense of awe for you and for your unsearchable mysteriousness. God, give us radical encounter!

> Abram had a radical encounter. When he came into contact with the divine, God changed his name to Abraham, and he fell on his face and became the father of nations (Gen. 17:3).

Jacob had a radical encounter. When he met a holy God and wrestled all night long with an angel, he left there with a blessing, a new name, and a limp to remind him of God's power and presence (Gen. 32:22–32).

Moses had a radical encounter. When he saw a burning bush that was not consumed, he fell in terror. He came to the bush a murderer and fugitive from justice, but he left a prophet and a deliverer (Ex. 3:1–14).

Ezekiel had a radical encounter. After admitting complete ignorance when asked, "Can these bones live?" he stood utterly transfixed before a valley of dry bones. Bone came upon bone, and flesh came upon flesh, and the breath of God brought the dead to life (Ezek. 37:1–14).

David had a radical encounter. After hiding his sin with Bathsheba, he was confronted by the prophet Nathan, who pulled the covers off and said, "Thou art the man" (2 Sam. 12:7, KJV). In complete contrition, David wrote, "Create in me a clean heart, O God; and renew a right spirit within me" (Ps. 51:10, KJV).

Peter, James, and John had a radical encounter. They thought they were on their way to a regular prayer meeting, but to their amazement they discovered when they arrived that Jesus' clothes shone like the sun and he had fellowship with Elijah and Moses. They wanted to stay up there and build three booths and worship (Mt. 17:1–4).

Saul had a radical encounter. He was on his way to persecute the church and kill Christians when he was knocked off his horse and blinded by the divine light, and instead of continuing to persecute, he became an evangelist (Acts 9:1–19).

And guess what? God has a radical encounter for you. The awesome glory of a mysterious God and holy God can break out at any time, in any place, and for anybody who is sensitive to the Spirit's urging. God is about to break forth right now. God is about to reveal divine purpose and divine mission right now. God is asking, "Is there anyone who will go for us, right now? Is there anybody who will say, 'Here am I, Lord, send me?' Does anyone want to be made holy? Does anybody want a radical encounter with the holy?" Be God right here and right now. Be holy. Hallowed be thy name. Break up our trivialities, our casual spiritual experiences, our perfunctory and obligatory worship. Break up the yawn of our familiarity and deliver radical encounter. Be God today. Thank you for not being a manageable deity. Thank you for not allowing yourself to be trivial. Thank you for cutting through our illusions. Break out! Break forth! Break in! We petition you. Hallowed be thy name.

Note

[1]Donald W. McCullough, *The Trivialization of God: The Dangerous Illusion of a Manageable Deity* (Colorado Springs: NavPress), 1995.

God's Government in the Human Heart

"Thy kingdom come" (Mt. 6:10)

We talk a whole lot about the church, but we don't talk much about the kingdom. We talk a lot about the size of churches, and the number of members, and the size of the budget, and the latest and greatest preachers, but we don't talk much about the kingdom. We talk about money, programs, status, grapevines, and gossip, but we don't talk much about the kingdom. We sound much like the disciples, who thought that Jesus was referring to a political kingdom when he announced that the kingdom had come. They expected an earthly empire that would chase out the oppressive Romans and establish Israel as the leading nation in the world. They thought that Jesus was going to institute a political kingdom that would usher in the age of blessing for Israel. When their political vision for the kingdom was deferred at Calvary, they were forced to understand the kingdom of God in broader terms. But it was not until the Holy Spirit fell on Pentecost that they got a true understanding or a liberating glimpse of the kingdom of God.

Though we, like Jesus' first disciples, don't talk much about the kingdom, that is pretty much all that Jesus talks about. According to Mark 1:14, Jesus came into Galilee preaching the good news of the kingdom of God. Mark says that at the very beginning and inaugural point of Jesus' ministry, Jesus is talking about the kingdom. Luke 4:43 records Jesus' words: "I must preach the good news of the kingdom of God to the other towns also, because that is why I was sent." Jesus went through every city and every village preaching and demonstrating the good news of the kingdom of God. He said:

> *"But seek first his kingdom and his righteousness, and all these things will be given to you as well" (Mt. 6:33).*
>
> *"The knowledge of the secrets of the kingdom of heaven has been given to you" (Mt. 13:11).*
>
> *"You are not far from the kingdom of God" (Mk. 12:34, one of my favorites).*
>
> *"The kingdom of God does not come with your careful observation, nor will people say, 'Here it is,' or 'There it is,' because the kingdom of God is within you" (Lk. 17:20).*

Jesus talked about the kingdom of God more than he talked about anything else.

The kingdom is based in the paradoxical name and nature of God. By paradoxical I mean that because two sides of life can be true at the same time, one has to live somewhere in the middle. In other words, the kingdom of God is preached and therefore inaugurated; it is here, but it is also on the way. That's what paradoxical means. Two things that seem opposite can be simultaneously true, so we live in the middle. The kingdom is here. It has already been preached. It has already been inaugurated. It is here; yet it is still on the way. The kingdom is plain, but it is also mysterious. The kingdom is open to everybody, but it is also hidden. Paradoxical. Though it somehow is never fully realized, it is so profound and so real that we cannot escape its claim. The church is the kingdom in its visible and fallible form; though the church is fallible, it is still the kingdom of God. The kingdom is the most beautiful and the most alluring thing in life, yet the kingdom is also the most demanding and the most challenging thing in life. God will have purity even if God has to burn us clean. God will have truth in our lives even if God has to make us hurt like a demon to get that truth out of us. This kingdom of love and peace and joy is the most beautiful thing that the world ever has known. But it is challenging. And it is demanding. And it is exacting. The kingdom of God is paradoxical.

The kingdom of God is God's reign, not over a country or a group of people, but over the whole of human history. This kingdom of God affirms what is good, true, and just in every age, and it corrects what is misguided, unjust, and wrong. God's kingdom is not about a geographical country, nor a particular race or ethnicity. God's kingdom does not settle on boundaries that we make, such as a particular version of the Christian faith that we endorse (as if we have the right to exclude others who do not happen to agree with us). The kingdom of God is not about a sentimental vagueness that does not require anything of us except that we try to be nice. The kingdom of God is not a national or a political kingdom, but a community in God's care that lives in love, joy, peace, and righteousness.

The kingdom of God is under divine sovereignty. *The kingdom of God is God's government set up in the human heart.* When we pray, "Thy kingdom come," we're saying, "God, set up your government in our lives. God, set up your government in our church. God, set up your government in our nation and world." When we pray, "Thy kingdom come," we're saying, "God, come into a person's heart at the point of regeneration to make that heart a holy habitation." When we say, "Thy kingdom come," we're asking the living God to so invade lives that God's authority would be established in persons' minds and wills. When we pray, "Thy kingdom come," we are asking God to set up government in the human life and heart.

When we say, "Thy kingdom come," we understand the human being as a temple, an abode, a residence of the Most

High, a place where God can reside; a place where God can set up shop; a place where God can set up divine activity; a place that God can occupy. Only when God occupies a heart can it be said that the kingdom has come to earth. So there is only as much kingdom in any church as the members allow God to set up government in their hearts. It is not in the church constitution. It is not in the buildings. It is not how new or how old the edifice is, or how long one has been a member. It is not your leadership position or your status. It is whether or not you allow God to set up God's government in your heart. And unless we are willing to let God fully set up God's government in our lives, it's factitious to pray this prayer. If we are not willing to let God establish God's government in our churches, then we are playing church when we pray, "Thy kingdom come." "Thy kingdom come" means, "God, set up your reign, your rule, and your sovereignty in the human heart."

I asked the question, "God, how does your government get set up in a human heart?" And the response came, "The human heart must desire it." The kingdom of God does not come by force. The kingdom of God does not come by politics. The kingdom of God does not come by backroom deals. The kingdom does not come by a political vote. The kingdom of God is a reality that only comes by our choice because we desire it to come, because we want it to come, because we pray for it to come, because we thirst for it to come. That is the only way that it comes. Jesus does not come to the human heart by force or domination or manipulation. Jesus comes by invitation. The kingdom of God will only come to our churches by invitation. The fullness of God's presence cannot be manipulated, tricked, or made up. It only comes when it is truly invited by a people who desire and thirst for the kingdom to come.

I asked God, "How do we get to the place that we truly desire for the kingdom to be set up in the human heart?" And God replied, "You have to be tired of the pain of your old lifestyle. You have to be sick and tired of being sick and tired." You must move beyond blaming other people. If your family is sick, you are probably contributing to the sickness. So the kingdom of God only comes when you stand in the family and say, "I am tired of the family being sick, and this is how I have contributed to the sickness." The kingdom doesn't come when you blame other people. It doesn't come when you point out other folks' problems. The kingdom only comes when you ask God to change your heart. That's why John the Baptist says, "Repent ye, for the kingdom of heaven is at hand" (Mt. 3:2, KJV). Repent.

We need a time of repentance. We need a time with ashes on our foreheads. We need to do as the Israelites did and tear off our clothes and ask God to forgive us, for we've fallen short of God's glory. We need to fall on our faces before God. We need corporate congregational repentance. That's the whole body repenting; nobody can escape. We need individual repentance, which means that some individuals in the corporate body need to get up and repent. After that, we need clergy repentance so that the clergy aren't just giving the word of God without needing the very word that they are giving to other people. We need church leaders' and officers' repentance. Leaders need to say, "I'm sorry." Leaders need to apologize to each other, to God, and to the church. Then the members ought to get up and apologize and admit they haven't done what they were supposed to do, and they haven't been what they were supposed to be. We all need to fall on our faces and ask God to set up God's government. We need to ask God to have God's way and do God's own thing, and to be God all by God's self. When we get to the point of repentance, guess what? The kingdom of God is at hand.

God says, "When you repent, I will come and set up my reign." God says, "Some of you all think the church is a democracy. It's not that. A democracy moves according to the will of the people. This is a theocracy." We move according to the will of God, and it is the people's responsibility to seek the will of God. It is the people's job to agree with God's will. That's the difference between a theocracy and a democracy. Democracy means the people canvass the room to decide if they have enough votes to get their agenda done. Oh, but that's not what we are talking about. We are talking about getting on your face and petitioning, "God, make your agenda plain. God, have your way in this place. God, I want to be in agreement with what you are doing." We don't have to invent God's work. We don't have to make up God's work. God is already at work. We just want to join where God is busy. The will of the people is only legitimate if it lines up with the will of God. And God says, "If you repent, I shall come and set up a government. And when I come and set up my government, then peace and joy shall reign." Isaiah 9:6 says,

> For unto us a child is born, unto us a son is given: and the **government** shall be upon his shoulder: and his name shall be called Wonderful, Counsellor, The mighty God, The everlasting Father, the Prince of Peace. Of the increase of his **government** and peace there shall be no end, upon the throne of David, and upon his kingdom, to order it, and to establish it with justice from henceforth even for ever. The zeal of the LORD of hosts will perform this. (KJV)

Look at the second chapter of Isaiah, verse 2:

> And it shall come to pass in the last days, that the mountain of the LORD'S house shall be established in the top of the mountains, and shall be exalted above the hills; and all nations shall flow into it. And many people shall go and say, Come ye, and let us go up to the mountain of the LORD, to the house of the God of Jacob; and he will teach us of his ways, and we will walk in his paths, for out of Zion shall go forth the law, and the word of the LORD from Jerusalem. And he shall judge among the nations, and shall rebuke

many people: and they shall beat their swords into plowshares, and their spears into pruning hooks: nation shall not lift up sword against nation, neither shall they learn war any more. (KJV)

When God sets up government, then peace shall reign. When God sets up government, then we shall beat our swords into plowshares. When God sets up government, then we shall study war no more. For unto us a child is born and unto us a son is given. And his name shall be called Wonderful, Counselor, The Mighty God, The Everlasting Father, and The Prince of Peace. We know him as Jesus. And here is the one of whom Isaiah prophesied, praying in Matthew 6, "Thy kingdom come."

Do you remember your civics lessons? When I was in eighth grade you could not get your diploma unless you passed a civics exam. One of the questions they asked was: What is the function of government? The function of government is to provide justice, maintain domestic order and security, and protect from outside attack. Another question was: How many branches of government are there? There are three branches of government—legislative, executive, and judicial. When God sets up government in the human heart, God says, "I have a legislative branch"—God the Father and the Creator. God makes all the laws that govern time and space, human behavior, and human relationships. "Then I have an executive branch," God says. "It's run by President Jesus. Mr. Bush is the President of the United States, but I have a President higher than Mr. Bush. Then I have a judicial branch. The Chief Justice of the Supreme Court is the Holy Spirit." God says, "I will set up my government." God says, "I will offer you services when my government gets in place. I will establish justice. That's what I'll do. I will maintain domestic order and security. I will protect you from outside attacks and even if outside attacks come, I shall prosper you in the attack."

God says, "I have a constitution I want you to live by. It is called the Bible. My government runs according to this constitution." God says, "I have a government, and I have embassies around the world. They are called local churches. My embassies have ambassadors, and they are called pastors." God says, "If you are a citizen of my kingdom, then you have to pay taxes. And guess what? Your tithe is the tax that you pay to the kingdom." God says, "I even have a pledge of allegiance to my kingdom. It is called the Lord's Prayer":

> Our Father who art in heaven, Hallowed be thy name. Thy kingdom come. Thy will be done on earth, as it is in heaven. Give us this day our daily bread, and forgive us our trespasses as we forgive those who trespass against us. And lead us not into temptation, but deliver us from evil. For thine is the kingdom, and the power, and the glory forever.

Well, I don't know about you, but I pledge allegiance to this kingdom. I give God glory in this kingdom. I am a member of this kingdom. I am saved by this Savior. I am delivered by Jesus. He is my President. And the Holy Spirit is my Supreme Court. Let the kingdom come. Let the kingdom come in me. Let it come in us. Let the kingdom come. Let us all who can and are willing stand and place our hands on our hearts and recite together our pledge of allegiance. Our Father who art in heaven...

On Earth as in Heaven

"Thy will be done on earth, as it is in heaven" (Mt. 6:10)

Twenty-five years ago, I stood in front of an altar and heard these words: "Wilt thou take this woman to be your lawful, wedded wife, to live according to God's holy ordinances in the holy estate of matrimony? Forsaking all others, will you be hers and hers alone? If so, say, 'I will.'" And I said, "I will." What did I really mean when I said, "I will"? I, Frank Anthony Thomas, as a human being created by God, have a will, and I commit it to a marriage relationship with this woman until death. It was voluntary. I was not under force or compulsion. I was not under legal obligation. I, all by myself, said, "I will." I did not need my parents. I was of age, and I could speak for myself. I did it without a grudge, and I was not under any constraint. I committed my intentions, my future, and my purpose in partnership with this woman. I asserted myself and was decisive and said, "I will."

In our text, which is the fifth petition of the Lord's Prayer, Jesus prays for God's will when he says, "Thy will be done." It was clear to Jesus that just as I have a will, God has a will. What do we mean when we say that God has a will? *First, God has a mind such that God thinks and God reasons:* "I know the **thoughts** that I **think** toward you, saith the LORD" (Jer. 29:11, KJV). "My **thoughts** are not your thoughts" (Isa. 55:8). "'Come now, let us **reason together**,' says the LORD"

(Isa. 1:18). *Second, God has emotions, and God feels*: "For God so **loved** the world, that [God] gave [the] only begotten Son, that whosoever believeth in him should not perish, but have everlasting life" (Jn. 3:16, KJV). "How great is the **love** the Father has lavished on us" (1 Jn. 3:1). "God is love"(1 Jn. 4:16). God loves and God feels toward us. Third, *God has plans and intentions*. God **chooses**, and God **decides** directions and courses of actions. God **intends**, that is God purposes and plans. "You did not **choose** me, but I **chose** you" (Jn. 15:16). "'I know the plans I have for you,' sayeth the Lord…'Plans to give you a hope and a future'" (paraphrase of Jer. 29:11). God has a mind, emotions and feelings, and plans and intentions, which is to say that God has a will. God's will is expressed in God's decisiveness and God's assertiveness. God wills.

Jesus further explains in the prayer in our text, "Thy will be done on earth as it is in heaven," that in heaven, God's will is perfectly done. In heaven, God's purposes and plans are already fulfilled. In heaven, God's intention is already carried out. God's government is already established in heaven. What does God's government look like? It almost looks like a democracy, but it really is not where the people collectively express their will through vote. In a democracy, the people have a will, and the will of the people shapes governmental plans and intentions. But God's government is a theocracy. In a theocracy, the goal of the government, the goal of the people, is to submit to the will of God. God rules heaven by the ethic of submission to God's will. Heaven only acts to fulfill the will of God. Heaven is run by submission to the will of God.

Jesus makes it plain when he prays, "Thy will be done on earth as it is in heaven," that the earth is the place where God's will is not fully done. The earth is the place where there is a lack of submission to the will of God. Why is there a lack of submission to the will of God here? Human beings have a will. Human beings have their own intentions. It is called free will. Human beings have the right to act on their own initiatives without force, compulsion, or constraint. My human will is free, and I can commit it to the causes and purposes that I choose. I can commit my will to marriage or I can commit my will to singleness. I can commit my will to good or I can commit my will to evil. I can commit my will to God or I can commit that will against God. I am a free moral agent, and I have a free will.

On earth, many of us commit our will against God. When I commit my will against God, it is called rebellion, or sin. Often we have a will that stands against God's will. I believe we stand our will against the will of God because we are full of will. We refuse to acknowledge that we are not God. We indulge our capacity as a free moral agent and act as if we were God.

Les Farber taught that human beings are very often full of will, or willful. He taught that being willful is the refusal to acknowledge the limitations of being human in this life, and therefore, in my words, we play God. He said there are certain things that we do not have any control over, and we have to accept that accomplishment of them is beyond our will. For example, he would say,

one can will sitting at the dinner table, but one cannot will appetite;

one can will going to bed, but one cannot will sleep;

one can will the family being together, but one cannot will togetherness.

When we are willful, we act as if we could will sleep or will the family to truly be together in unity and harmony. When we are willful, we act as if we had control over more than we have control over. Farber acknowledged three fundamental limits in life: There are limits to our time—we will all die. There are limits to our knowledge—when we become educated, we become aware of how much we really do not know. There are limits to our power—we cannot make anyone do anything. To be willful is to ignore the limits. When people are being full of will, they are violating one, if not more, of these three, and acting in the position of God. God is the only one who is unlimited in knowledge, time, and power. God's will has a difficult time getting done on earth because we are exaggerating our time, power, or knowledge and accomplishing our will.

Often we have such an exaggerated sense of the importance of our will that we attempt to make other people follow our will. And when we attempt to make other people follow our will, then we are in a battle of wills. The world is full of battles of will: the tragedy of warfare either ethnically or religiously based; tension between two colleagues, two coworkers, a husband and wife, or a parent and a child. In our sin and rebellion against God, where we have the audacity to play God, we have many wars of wills

But Jesus prayed for God's will and that our will or willfulness would be overcome. Jesus prayed that we would know the limitations of our time, knowledge, and power. Jesus prayed that we would learn that we are not God and that God is still God. It is only when we accept the limits of our knowledge, power, and time that are we in a position to submit to God. It is only when we truly acknowledge our limits that we can say, "Thy will be done." Jesus was teaching us to say, "Lord, I commit my will to thy will. I do not want my will to be done, but I submit my will to thy will, and thy will be done. Thy will be done on earth as it is in heaven. Thy will be accomplished." Jesus said, "For I came down from heaven, not to do mine own will, but the will of him that sent me" (Jn. 6:38, KJV).

I do not want to pretend that the submission of the human will to the will of God is a very easy thing. Often, submission to God's will is painful. Jesus was on his way to die at Calvary. He knew that death was imminent and yet he prayed in Gethsemane, "Take this cup." Sometimes the will of God will take us into some difficult and painful places.

Sometimes the will of God will interrupt the plans that we have for our own lives and take us into some directions that we prefer not to choose. But Jesus was able to acknowledge his limits and submit. Jesus concludes the matter with "not my will, but thy will be done." Jesus, as a human being created by God, had a will, and he committed it to God, even if it meant death. It was voluntary. He was not under force or compulsion. He was not under legal obligation. He, all by himself, said, "Thy will be done." He did not need his parents. He was of age and could speak for himself. He did it without a grudge, and he was not under any constraint. He committed his intentions, future, and purpose in submission to God. He asserted himself and was decisive as a free moral agent and said, "Thy will be done." God's will was done on earth as it was in heaven.

Feed Me till I Want No More

"Give us this day our daily bread"
(Mt. 6:11)

On Thursday, October 11, 2001, the Mississippi Boulevard Christian Church family offered $100 in cash to each person who was laid off at the Memphis International Airport as a result of the World Trade Center tragedy. We wanted to do our part to help with the "collateral damage" from the tragedy of 9–11–01. Four hundred and five people came through our doors, and we gave freely, generously, and lovingly to each one of them. We also prayed for them, counseled with those who wanted it, and gave them overwhelming love, support, and acceptance.

I greeted some of the people as they came in and as they left. I said to one young man, "I wish we could do more. I wish we could fix it and make everything all right, but we can't fix it because we don't have the capacity, and so what we're doing is giving 'daily bread'". And when I said "daily bread," I realized that we were giving people bread for that day. I realized that we were offering ministry to people in the spirit of Jesus in the Lord's Prayer, "Give us this day our daily bread."

The beginning of the text in Matthew 6:11 says: "Give us." First of all, "Give us" is addressed to the Giver. Jesus acknowledges that God is the Giver, that God supplies the earth's natural resources for our nourishment. God supplies the rain and the sunshine, the water and the air, and all the things that provide life on this planet. Even our ability to work and earn food comes from God's hand. It has nothing to do with our ability to think. It has nothing to do with our training. Our ability to think is from God. If any of us have the ability to do math and numbers as an accountant, that's from God. If any of us can write, paint pictures, sing, or make music, that's all from God. If you can supervise, manage, and organize, that's all from God. If you know how to fix things and can use a screwdriver and hammer, if you know how to roll and bake cookies, if you know how to interpret law books, it is all from God. I don't care what it is. God is the context that allows you to earn a living and eat.

You cannot force God; you must ask, "Give us." Asking is a sign of humility. The prayer does not say that you **take** your daily bread. It does not say that you are **entitled to** your daily bread. It does not say that you are to **demand** your daily bread. As if any of us would have the audacity to go to God and say: "God, you owe me my daily bread. Give me my daily bread!" No. It's a petition; it's a prayer; it's a beseeching; it's a request. Give unto us. Please. Give us our daily bread. If you don't give it, we won't have any. God, we come with open palms for you to give. God, we beseech you to be compassionate and merciful. God, we ask. Give us our daily bread.

The Lord responds, "Ask and it will be given to you; seek and you will find; knock and the door will be opened to you...Which of you, if his son [or daughter] asks for bread, will give him a stone? Or if he asks for a fish, will give him a snake? If you, then, though you are evil, know how to give good gifts to your children, how much more will your Father in heaven give good gifts to those who ask him!" (Mt. 7:7, 9–11). God in God's infinite wisdom and tender mercy gives us our daily bread.

Second, let us look at the word *daily.* Daily reflects the precarious lifestyle of many first-century workers who were paid one day at a time; a few days of illness or a few days of layoff could spell disaster for their families. They weren't paid on the fifteenth and the thirtieth as many of us. They were paid daily. They worked the day and they got their pay at the end of the day. They were paid **daily**. Daily is a very precious word, an urgent word, and a needful word when you receive what you need to feed your family at the end of each and every day. Daily means something when you live hand to mouth at the end of each day.

The Greek word for daily is *epiousias* (ep-ee-OO-see-us). One of the ways we discover what a biblical word means is that we look up as many verses of scripture as we can to see how it is used in various contexts. We can reach a reasonably accurate conclusion about what the word means based on the various contexts. But the word *epiousias* is only used twice in the entire New Testament. It is used once in Matthew's recording of the Lord's Prayer, and again in Luke's version of the prayer. Therefore, without a lot of verses to compare, the best that scholars can understand, e*piousias* simply means daily.

Though the meaning of the word seems simple and direct, biblical scholars have nevertheless struggled with how to translate *epiousias*. The Coptic church's translation is "Give us our bread for tomorrow." The Bohairic translation is "Give us the bread that is needful for each day." The Latin Vulgate gave us the word *daily.* Give us this day our daily bread. Give us the bread that is sufficient for this day.

Scholars postulate that when Jesus said "daily," he was thinking of Exodus 16:15, which records the Israelites in the wilderness yearning for food. They were in the wilderness looking for food, and God rained down manna from heaven. They had never seen manna. They didn't know what manna was. They were astonished because each and every morning there was fresh manna from above. Right away they discovered that they could not horde or store up manna. All they could do was take enough for each day. They couldn't pile it up in their tents and then sell it to other people. They could only get what their families needed. Everyone only could receive *daily* bread.

I believe the word *daily* stands against the excessive need for security and safety that tempts us in our human living. We have health insurance, car insurance, home insurance, apartment insurance, life insurance, death insurance, and rainy day insurance. We have 401(k)s, 403(b)s, savings accounts, mutual funds, tax shelters, and stock portfolios. We do financial planning to ensure that we are able to retire. We are concerned about the level of equity in our homes, the death benefit on our insurance. We are concerned about making out our wills and about how our inheritance is going to be divided. We are concerned, as we should be, about all these things, but the word *daily* stands as a corrective and a warning. The word *daily* suggests that we be careful lest when wealth multiplies and we begin to imagine ourselves as self-sufficient, we think we are independent of God. But *daily* means that you are cognizant that you live hand to mouth. You are aware that things could change quickly. Layoff notices could come. The company could not make any money. You realize that you are living life daily. *Daily* means that you trust more in "Every good gift and every perfect gift is from above, and cometh down from the Father of lights" (Jas. 1:17, KJV) than in education, connections, and money.

And last, let us look at bread: Give us this day our daily bread. Bread is the food of poor people. Bread is not luxury food. In biblical days meat was only available for the wealthy. The only way poor people got meat was by buying the meat left over from animals that were sacrificed at the temple. But they had that opportunity infrequently because animals weren't sacrificed every day, which meant that poor people didn't have much meat, so bread constituted the basic meal. Bread was symbolic of the basic dietary staple of the majority of people on the planet.

Bread is the symbol of sustenance for the poor. We have enough bread on our planet, but we have distribution problems relative to our bread because some people store bread up in barns and charge money, and if you can't pay, you can't eat. This means that some of us end up with a whole lot of bread, and others end up with nothing. Those of us living in the United States with plenty of bread need to ask fundamental questions about why we have so much while others have so little. The truth is that everyone could eat were it not for the distribution problem. God takes a revolutionary position on bread distribution, offering bread free of charge to everyone. God says, "You who have no money, come, buy and eat!" (Isa. 55:1). God does not have a distribution problem; sin entangles us, and we block up the distribution chain. When we gave $100 to everybody who came through the door that had lost an airport job as a result of 9–11–01, we were distributing bread in the spirit of Isaiah 55:1.

And when we attempt to distribute bread such that they who have no money can come, buy, and eat, God gets involved. As I was preparing the people for the distribution, I made a major mathematical mistake. I calculated that if we gave five hundred people $100 each, that would be $5,000. I was pretty sure that we could financially afford what we were proposing to do, and so I was at peace when I announced it to the church. One of our ministers called me and said, "Pastor Thomas, you have made a huge mistake. Five hundred people at $100 per person is $50,000." And I said, "I have a headache. I'm going to bed. I'll talk to you tomorrow." So I came to work on Monday, and we had a meeting to discuss our options. *Option Number One*: give until the money ran out. We had enough money for two hundred people, and when we had given to two hundred people, we would turn everyone else away. *Option Number Two*: cut the gift for each person to $50, and we could serve more people. But we had called a press conference and already announced to the community that we were going to give $100. *Option Number*

Three: pray and trust God to meet the need however many came. So we had prayer. After we prayed, we decided on *Option Number Three*, sent the chief financial officer to the bank to get funds for five hundred people and said, "We're moving on faith. God will have to do it."

That following Thursday, October 11, I arrived at church at about by 8:00 a.m., and people were already lined up all around the walls. My flesh wanted to start worrying. The people kept coming, and the people kept coming, and the needs were multiplying. The chief financial officer went upstairs and got some more money and brought it back, and some more money again as the people continued to come and come. We served four hundred and five people. God allowed a donor to give us exactly enough for the extra two hundred people. After the contribution, we all cried and prayed. I kept saying, "I have never seen the righteous forsaken or their children begging bread" (Ps. 37:25). Others rejoiced and joined in and said, "Cast your bread upon the waters and see if it won't come back to you" (paraphrase of Ecc. 11:1). We learned that when we do what God says to do, God will make provision. If you put God first, you won't have to beg for bread.

This is the promise: Any church that puts God first will never beg for bread. Any man or woman who puts God's agenda first is bound to have bread. It might be daily bread. You might not have 401(k) bank bread. You might not have 403(b) retirement fund bread. You might not have big bread. But oh, you shall have the bread that is needful for this day. Scholars think that *epiousias* was a word used to describe the experience of obtaining what is needful. Get God's agenda. When we get around God's table with God's agenda, we get what's needful. God doesn't always give you the full plan. God doesn't always show you what God is doing with you. God doesn't always show you what God is taking you through. Oh, but you will have daily bread.

Bread is the person of Jesus. "I am the bread of life," he says in John 6:48. "I am the living bread that came down from heaven" (Jn. 6:51). Well, what did he mean? What is bread? Bread is composed of kernels of wheat grain that are broken, crushed, bruised, and ground into fine flour. The flour is then mixed with salt, water, and yeast, then kneaded and shaped into a loaf that rises. After the loaf rises, it is baked until it turns a beautiful golden brown. Once it comes out of the oven and cools off, that which was once grain provides life to those who eat it. The life of the wheat is transmitted to human beings through the process of death, subsequent resurrection, and final assimilation by the body. We take bread, we do eat, and we do live.

Oh, a similar process has made the life of God in Christ available to us. Our savior became God's grain. Jesus was wheat that was crushed and milled and made into flour. God added the yeast, and Jesus was kneaded and shaped, and he rose. He was put in an oven on Friday, where he stayed all night and all day Saturday. Oh, but early on Sunday morning, he was a golden brown, and he came out of that grave, putting one foot on earth and the other on heaven, saying, "Now all power is in my hand, and nobody that eats of me shall ever die. Nobody that partakes of me shall ever go hungry. Anybody that takes of my sustenance, will always have enough." Because of this, we proclaim that Jesus is the Bread of Life. We ask the bread of life to give us our daily bread. In the words of a familiar hymn, "Bread of heaven, feed me till I want no more! Bread of heaven, feed me till I want no more!"[1]

> *Guide me, O thou great Jehovah,*
> *Pilgrim through this barren land;*
> *I am weak, but Thou art mighty,*
> *Hold me with thy powerful hand:*
> *Bread of Heaven, Bread of Heaven,*
> *Feed me till I want no more;*
> *Feed me till I want no more.*

Bread of heaven, give me what I need. Give me the bread that is sufficient for this day. Give us our daily bread!

Note

[1]William Williams, "Guide Me, O Thou Great Jehovah" (1745).

Spirituality and Religion

"Forgive us our debts, as we forgive our debtors" (Mt. 6:12)

Many people are very good at the first part of this petition in the Lord's Prayer: "forgive us our debts." We are very good at asking for forgiveness from God. Most of us acknowledge that we are not sufficient in and of ourselves to run our lives, to control our lives, and that we need some help outside ourselves if our lives are going to be meaningful. Most of us are religious. Religion is the belief in a Supreme Being, in God. Most of us acknowledge that we believe in God and have some form of allegiance to God, and admit that God can help us in our lives.

As a part of religion, we go to church, and we put a couple of dollars in the plate to help the church. As a part of our religious duty, many of us work in the church. Many of us use religious language, carry around religious books, and buy religious music. As a part of religious ritual, we take communion. It is even possible to practice religion and become a leader in the church. It is possible to practice religion and get ordained, be called Reverend, and even become a pastor to some people. Many people are religious.

Religion enables you to put a thin veneer of church over a non-regenerated life. Religion allows you to talk the Christian talk, but be unchanged and unredeemed at your core and in your soul. Religion lets you call on the name of God when you need or want something. Religion is for us and about us and will benefit us. We do not have a problem asking God for forgiveness. But because it is just religion, many of us will ask for forgiveness and then go out and do the same thing wrong again. Because it is just religion, it is not the deep repentance that will lead to growth. It is the shallow and surface rearrangement of the furniture to give the appearance of change, but in our hearts we are the same people. Religion is a thin veneer of church over a non-regenerated life. Religion is the thin veneer of propriety over an unchanged life.

The second section of this petition of the Lord's Prayer—"as we forgive"—deepens religion. "Forgive us as we forgive" is the concern of a regenerated life. To ask God for forgiveness is a normal and an average thing that we do on a regular basis, but it takes courage and strength for us to forgive someone else. "Forgive as we forgive" deepens and adds spirituality to religion.

I believe that the key test for spirituality is one's relationship with other people. I do not care how you make pronouncements about your vertical relationship with God. The measure of that vertical relationship is the quality of your horizontal relationships. You might be religious, you might show up to church, but that does not mean that you are spiritual. The quality of your relationships is a very significant indicator of the level of your spirituality. I believe that the bottom line of your spirituality is whether you have quality relationships with people. For example, how are you going to say that Jesus is a "heart fixer and a mind regulator" if you are not speaking to your mother? How can you say, "Jesus can make a way out of no way, can carve a tunnel of hope in the mountain of despair," if you walk down the other side of the church to avoid somebody who is standing on this side of the church? How can you say, "I love the Lord; God heard my cry and pitied my every groan," if you avoid your coworker or your fellow students? At the bottom of life is not wealth, looks, or degrees, but the quality of relationships that we foster and maintain.

The breakdown of human relationships is a very painful issue for many people. There are family members who are not talking to, but are talking about, other family members. There are fathers and mothers who have broken relationships; it is called divorce. Divorce is the acknowledgment that a relationship is broken. Some say drug, alcohol, and sexual abuse are results of broken relationship, but whether or not we agree with that, drug, alcohol, and substance abuse at a minimum create broken relationships. Neighbors fall out of relationship on the same block; coworkers fall out of relationship in the same workspace.

Even in the church there are broken relationships. There are people who do not like each other and have not forgiven each other. Some people have held grudges and shut each other out. Some people judge issues based not on merit, fact, or what God would have done, but on whether or not they like the person who is raising the issue. It is called politics. And while we are engaging in broken relationships, religion makes us smile and be phony when we know we do not like each other. While we are engaging in broken relationships, religion makes us say good things up front in the public worship, but then spew venom and poison in the back on the grapevine. Religion makes us say one thing to one person and another thing to another person. Religion makes us praise Jesus together, then stab each other in the back after the benediction. Religion allows us to participate in communion together, disregarding our broken fellowship, knowing that Saint Paul said in 1 Corinthians 11:27–30 that some of us are sick because we eat and drink "unworthily." Paul meant that we eat and drink together with broken relationship. We've got our grudges. We are mad. We are upset. We don't like this, and we don't like that. And we don't like him, and we don't like her. And then on top of the thin veneer of religiosity, we have the audacity to ask God to forgive us our sins. Well, Jesus comes and brings a corrective.

This is a hard prayer because this part of the prayer is not about religion; it is about being spiritual. Jesus, when he prays the second part of the prayer, exposes the fact that forgiveness for many of us is so often about our own timetable. Jesus pulls the covers off the fact that we think it is about when we feel that we are ready to bury the hatchet. It is about forgiving only after we are satisfied with people's behavior. It is about our getting retribution before we forgive. It is about the person acting the way we want him or her to act and giving us the appropriate apology that we want to hear before we forgive. Jesus says regardless of your timetable, you will only be forgiven as you forgive.

Martin Luther King, Jr., sounded like Jesus when he asked this question: "Why are black people waiting for white people to repent before we forgive?" He asked that question. And then he explained it theologically. What he said was that our waiting doesn't follow biblically because the Bible says that while we were yet in our sins, Christ died. God did not wait for us to repent before God died, which means that reconciliation and forgiveness were available before we repented. So King asked, "Why are you all waiting on somebody else, black people? Why are you all waiting on white people to admit racism before you forgive them?" And then he said this. "Forgiveness only takes one." Why do you think forgiveness takes two? How were you forgiven? It took one, and his name was Jesus. While you were in the crack house, Christ died. While you were embezzling money, Christ died. While you were being recalcitrant and arrogant and ignorant, Christ died. While you were doing your dirt, Christ died. Forgiveness was already available for you to take advantage of even before you repented.

This text says that the same measure of judgment that you put on someone else, God is going to put on you. This text says that if you think that you need to be satisfied before you forgive, what do you think you have that will satisfy God before God forgives you? This text says be careful, because the same measure of mercy that you give is the measure that you will receive. I think the second part of this petition is critical because it is spiritual, *and as I heard Michael Eric Dyson say once, the role of spirituality is to make religion act right.*

Nothing is wrong with religion, but it is spirituality that makes religion act right. Nothing is wrong with going to church every Sunday, except that spirituality wants to deepen your being there. Spirituality wants to take religion to another level. It wants to make religion act right. Religion has at its base carnality, but spirituality has at its base the Spirit of God. The question is not whether you are a member of the church, but whether you have been born again. The question is not how long you have been an usher, but how long you have been saved, sanctified, and filled with the Holy Spirit. The issue is, what is the level of your spirituality?

What does the word *spiritual* mean? "Spirituality" is a quality that we become aware of in certain events, texts, persons, and places. *Spiritual* is a word that describes an event, text, person, or place that is holy, that participates in the realm of other-ness. To understand the word *spiritual* we must deal with the word *holy*. The root of the word *holy* is *whole* or *integer,* from which we get the word *integrity,* which means being whole without any breakage or fracture. It means being complete. Integrity means having no distinction between what you say in public and what you do in private. It is God's nature and God's character that is whole or holy. Holy is that which is other than us—something that is qualitatively different from everything that we know. And God has a realm, a kingdom, a reality that is as holy as God is. It is possible to live in this earthly realm that is not whole but participate in that other realm. "Spiritual" means to live in the awareness of the holy. Some people live in a stream of consciousness through which they avail themselves of the holy reality in our earthly reality. Who is the most spiritual person you know?

Who is that person who has the quality that is called "spirituality"? That person participates in the holy reality while walking and talking here on earth. *Spirituality is the holiness of the heavenly realm breaking forth and expressing itself through an event, text, person, or place on earth.*

I am saying that to be holy is to be able to forgive other people. I am saying that to be spiritual is to live in the awareness of the holy and to know that God will not forgive us unless we forgive other people. I am saying that in and of ourselves we cannot forgive. We are hurt too deeply. We are wounded, angry, bitter, disappointed, depressed, and hostile. We are not going to take it anymore. Some of us are out to hurt other people. We have been hurt, so we lash out and attempt to hurt others. We think that we can get by if we just focus on the first part of the petition that asks God for forgiveness. But that is religion, and what we are after is spirituality. It takes the Spirit of God to come in and bring the other reality into our lives to help us forgive. It takes the Spirit of God to come in and help us do what we cannot do easily by ourselves. God says, "I will help you, but let me continually remind you of one of the cardinal truths of this holy reality: if you do not forgive, you will not be forgiven." This is the spiritual reality. So because we want to be holy, we bury the hatchet, we put down the knife, we let go of the grudge, we extend mercy and grace called forgiveness. Forgiveness is the essence of spirituality and holy living.

Someone will undoubtedly say that "forgiveness is the essence of spirituality and holiness" is a strong statement. It is a strong statement, but I believe scripture backs it up. This concern is so important to Jesus that in Matthew 6:14–15 he reinterprets the entire Lord's Prayer through the lens of forgiveness. Jesus says:

> For if you forgive men when they sin against you, your heavenly Father will also forgive you. But if you do not forgive men their sins, your Father will not forgive your sins. (Mt. 6:14–15)

It is as if the teacher in concluding the lesson reinforces the most salient point as the final point of the lesson. Matthew comes back and reemphasizes the point just to make sure that you did not miss it: if you forgive others, God will forgive you; if you do not forgive others, God will not forgive you. To forgive deepens religion to the level of spirituality. Forgiveness is the essence of spirituality and holy living.

Spirituality says that if someone has something against you, leave your gift at the altar and go and be reconciled to your brother or sister (Mt. 5:23–24).

Spirituality answers the question "How many times should I forgive my brother?" with the reply "seventy times seven" (Mt. 18:21–22).

Spirituality says, "bless those who curse you, pray for those who mistreat you" (Lk. 6:28).

Spirituality says, "Be ye not weary in well doing, because you will reap a harvest if you faint not" (paraphrase of Gal. 6:9).

Spirituality says, "Forgive us our debts, as we forgive our debtors" (Mt. 6:12, KJV).

Of Trials and Tests

"Lead us not into temptation"
(Mt. 6:13)

The Greek word for temptation—*peirasmos (peer-AS-mose)*—is more closely translated, "Lead us not into trials," or "Lead us not into tests." Testing as consistent with *peirasmos* means to be put into a situation for refinement, to be put in a situation to prove your strength or your character, to be put in a situation where you are enticed to sin. Enticing you to sin is one way to test you. In other words, you can be tested and achieve greater purity. You can be tested and develop greater self-confidence. You can be tested and grow in the faith. Even if we fail the test by sinning, the test (not the sin) can still lead to growth in faith, purity, and self-confidence. Sinning itself may motivate us to seek God's strength to overcome. Temptation occurs when you sin in the midst of the test. Temptation is a response to a trial or a test by succumbing to sin.

Temptation focuses on our want or desire for something that we know is not right or good for us, such as cigarettes. You can put a package of cigarettes in front of me, and it is no temptation for me. As a matter of fact, you can pile cigarettes all the way up to my head, and it won't mean a thing to me because I do not **want** cigarettes. A key element of a temptation is that you have to **want or desire** the temptation that is offered. I have smoked one cigarette in my life. I happened to be in the seventh grade when I smoked it. When I got through gagging and coughing, I did not think a cigarette and gagging and coughing were cool. Therefore, I have not had the want or the desire for a cigarette since. So you can pile cigarettes in front of me all you want, but I will not be tempted because I do not want them.

Now, what most of us do is brag about how spiritually strong we are in areas that don't tempt us in the first place. What we keep quiet about are the things that we would break out in a cold sweat over if they were placed in front of us. Temptation has to do with really wanting something that you are not supposed to have or that is not good for you. Temptation has to do with the desire for forbidden fruit. Temptation has to do with the excessive desire for fame or popularity. Temptation has to do with the excessive want for power or pleasure. Temptation has to do with an inordinate desire for a forbidden woman or man. Temptation has to do with an extreme need for money, silver, gold, and for expensive toys and trinkets. These are the things of temptation.

Hebrews 2:18 says that Jesus was tempted in all things just as we are, so he is therefore able to comfort us in our temptation. I like this verse because Jesus had to **want and desire** for something to have been a temptation. If he had not wanted it, it would not have been a temptation. Understanding this, I get tired of the namby-pamby, cotton candy Jesus that we drag out on Sunday mornings in church. I get tired of this Jesus who is so spiritual that there is no way that he could have had sexual desire. This Jesus was so busy looking at heaven that he never looked at the earthly pleasures around him. The Bible says that Jesus was tempted in all ways that we are tempted; therefore, Jesus had to want and desire just as we want and desire.

Now, there is a difference between Jesus and us. The Bible also says that when we are tempted, God will provide an emergency exit (1 Cor. 10:13). So it wasn't that Jesus did not have desire or want some of the same things that we want; Jesus simply was a master of the emergency exit. He took every off ramp before he got in trouble. He exited every side ramp so he could live holy in the midst of the same things that you and I desire. The miracle was not that Jesus did not have desires for some of the women around him who were very attractive. The miracle was that though he was tempted, he never touched anybody. That's the miracle. The miracle is to have desire, but to streamline it into a holy life. The miracle is to have desire, but to give it to God and allow God to give you avenues of escape. You can desire and still be holy. You just have to learn to take the emergency exit. A lot of us pass up that exit. We have our eyes so focused on what we want that we pass up the emergency exit. But Jesus, who went through every temptation just as you and I do, was victorious, and because he was victorious he can assist us when we are tempted, when we are in trouble, when we are about to succumb—because he has been through it and has already been victorious.

The Greek *peirasmos* does not only mean to be enticed to sin. It also implies a trial or a testing. A trial is a test over an extended period of time. A trial is a test in which God is discerning your character. Cancer can be a trial; a lost job can be a trial; a divorce can be a trial; the death of a loved one can be a trial; widowhood can be a trial; the church can be a trial; persecution or ridicule can be a trial. **Trials have to do with different situations that we find ourselves in that test and measure our confidence in God.** You know you are in a trial when what you are going through tests your confidence in God.

In truth, a trial is something that we would rather avoid. We don't want our confidence in God tested. We don't want our earth shaken up. We don't want our world rearranged. We don't want our set agenda, our career plans, all messed up. A trial is something that we would rather avoid. A trial is a challenge to test what we are made of and ultimately to see what we believe.

Let's look at a real trial. In the early church era, when it was against the law to be a Christian and a person could undergo persecution for being one, the church worshiped in secret catacombs—Osama bin Laden-like caves. The police would hunt the Christians down, break into their secret meetings in the caves, and threaten, "If you don't say 'Caesar is Lord,' but persist in saying 'Jesus is Lord,' you will be lunch meat for the lions!" The police would then line the Christians up one by one, demanding that each one in turn declare whether Caesar or Jesus was Lord. No, you couldn't hide in your choir robes, and you couldn't hide in your preacher robes. You couldn't just say, "My mama was a great pillar of the truth in this church." You couldn't say that. You had to stand on your own. It didn't make any difference who you were or how long you had been a member of the church. The police would go one by one down the line: "Is Caesar Lord or is Jesus Lord?"

And guess what? Some of the folks responded, "Caesar is Lord." Imagine that. Imagine your being in the church, serving with somebody who is faithfully handing out the communion cups Sunday after Sunday, weekend after weekend. And when the test comes, you go to the lions, and that person is still walking around. Or that person is your pastor, whom you have been serving and following, of whom you are proud. Suddenly, you are standing in line next to your pastor, and the pastor says, "Caesar is Lord." This is the real context of "once saved, always saved." We like to ask in sterile debate with our friends, "Are you once saved, always saved, or can you lose your salvation?" Well, the church in Hebrews (6:4–6) was especially upset because some of their people turned back, so the faithful ones declared, "If you turn back from the faith, then you must have never been saved in the first place because if you really know Jesus, you can't turn back. If you are really saved, you can't turn back." Turning back from the faith was so despicable to the faithful in the Hebrew church that they said the ones who turn back are "crucifying the Son of God all over again and subjecting him to public disgrace" (Heb. 6:6).

Jesus says, "Lead us not into temptation." Lead us not. Do you understand the sheer negativity? Lead us not. No, we don't want trials. No, we don't want tests. No, we don't want them. Lead us not. We don't want them because they are too difficult. They are too painful. We don't want them. Don't put us in situations where the true nature of our character must be revealed. Don't put us in those situations. We are nice church folks. We put on our nice, neat robes. We are serving God by giving God a couple of Sundays and a couple of days. Don't put us in situations where we have to decide if Christ is real or not. We don't want to go through trials and temptations. We don't want to have tests. We don't want to be put in a line where we have to answer either "Caesar is Lord" or "Jesus is Lord." We want to come to church and find nice, safe religion. We want our names to be on the roll of a certain church. We don't want to face times of trial. We don't want to go through heartache. We don't want to go through divorce. We don't want to go through cancer. We don't want to go through disease. Lead us not into times of extended temptation. We don't want it. It is like a future that we fear. We look at some trials and temptations and don't really believe that we can get to the other side.

Once my daughter slipped and fell and cut her lip in the front, and she had to get stitches. There was no anesthesia possible in this area inside the mouth between the inner lip and the gum of the mouth and lip, so she begged us not to send her behind the curtain and put her in the hands of the doctors. "Daddy, don't. Daddy, I don't want to go in there. I don't want to go through that," she pleaded. "Baby, but if you don't go through that, there won't be any healing," I contended. I told her, "This one is going to hurt. There is no way around it and no way to avoid it. This one is going to hurt." We stand around and tell God, "No, we don't want to go. We don't want that." And God says, "it is for your healing, but this one is going to hurt."

What is hard to accept is that we have to go through some things to get to our new future, and it is going to hurt. When we look at the hurt and the heartache, we say to God, "Lead us not into the pain to get to our new future. Lead us not into the struggle to get to the next level of life." Why would Jesus pray this? Why would Jesus pray, "Lead us not into temptation"? Jesus prayed this because we all pray it. Jesus was human just like us, and no human being willingly wants to deal with temptation and evil. It is human to feel that it would be better if we could get to the next level without the pain. That is what Jesus wishes in Gethsemane. He is saying, "I don't want the cup, but I'll drink from it if I have to." Jesus understood what he had to go through to take himself and us to the next level. Jesus understood how painful and difficult it would be, and how much he would have to give up (his life) to get us to the next place. He understood the price for us to receive salvation. He understood it and paid it.

"Lead us not into the struggle to get to the next level of life" is both what his prayer meant and not what it meant. The function of temptations and trials is to either launch you into or keep you from your future. In other words, the function of trials and temptations is to discern if you are ready for your new future or not. Sometimes through the trial we see that we do not belong to the future toward which we are headed. The trial has served as a warning and an eye-opener. It corrects a misstep. The test opens up our determination and gives us clarity about what is really important to us.

To get to the next level you have to go through some things. The more you go through, the higher the level you reach. If you are going through a lot right now, watch out. If you go through it with God and you let God try you and test you, you will face darkness and pain, but you will stand in your new future. At some point, you are going to have to give up all that you are for all that you might become. Becoming takes time. Becoming means that you are going to have to live in the darkness for awhile—live with some unanswered questions. But just make sure that you get a blessing out of all that you go through. A young preacher was pouring out his soul to Gardner C. Taylor, and after listening to his sad soliloquy, Dr. Taylor said, "Preacher, make sure that you don't go through all of that hurting for nothing." As a result of your trials, you ought to make some gain. Your prayer life ought to get deeper. Your faith ought to grow stronger. Your hope ought to be fortified; your testimony ought to be polished; and your religion ought to taste sweeter as a result of having gone through trials. Show me a person who has never gone through anything, and I will show you a person who has no power. You get power out of trials. I don't want it, and you don't want it, but that's where the power is. Lead us not into temptation.

The writer of James talks about trials and temptations in the context of joy. James 1:2–4 says,

> Consider it pure joy, my brothers, whenever you face trials of many kinds, because you know that the testing of your faith develops perseverance. Perseverance must finish its work so that you may be mature and complete, not lacking anything.

Count your trials, temptations, and tests as all joy. Jesus went through Gethsemane, came up to Calvary, was crucified, and lay dead in a tomb, but was raised to glory to sit at the right hand of God. And because he came through his trial victoriously, James says we can rejoice in any and all of our trials and temptations. James says we can "shout" through all our trials because these things develop perseverance and perseverance must finish its work so that you may be mature and complete. James says it is joy when you have all these things happen to you, because they only come to test your readiness for the next level. Go through whatever you have to go through to get to the next level. Stay with the process, James says, and go through whatever to get to your new future. James says that on the other side of the trial is a mature Christian character with the right kind of independence. Count it all as joy.

> *But this is joy that only God can give—*
> *joy that sees the rainbow of hope hanging on the clouds*
> *   of trouble—*
> *joy not because life is good but because God is good—*
> *joy because the cross is not greater than his grace and*
> *   the clouds cannot hide his blessed face—*
> *joy because trouble can't defeat you, death can't destroy*
> *   you, and the grave can't hold your body down—*
> *joy because your enemies can't prevail since if God is for*
> *   you, nobody can be against you—*
> *joy because truth crushed to earth will rise again—*
> *joy because the kingdom will come, God's will must be*
> *   done, every knee must bow, every tongue must*
> *   confess, every barrier must be broken—*
> *joy because weeping may endure for a night, but joy*
> *   comes in the morning—*
> *joy because one of these days the wicked shall cease from*
> *   troubling and the weary will be at rest—*
> *joy because the one that is in you is greater than*
> *   anything that is in the world—*
> *joy because nothing can separate you from the love of*
> *   God.*
> *Joy.*

Joy because God is at work in your life maturing and completing you so that you do not lack anything.

You Will Not Be Overcome

"Deliver us from evil" (Mt. 6:13)

Time magazine's person of the century was Albert Einstein.[1] The magazine used photographer Phillipe Halsman's legendary photo of Einstein for its cover. As he released the camera's shutter, Halsman asked Einstein, "So you don't believe there will ever be peace?" Halsman recalls that "Einstein's eyes had a look of immense sadness as well as a question and a reproach," and he answered, "No, as long as there is man there will be war." When the airplanes hit the twin towers of the World Trade Center on September 11, 2001, I knew in the depths of my soul that Einstein was correct. In this world, as long as human beings exist, there will be war.

War has been with us from the beginning of time and will be with us until its end. War is the human endeavor that has been waged on every continent and among every people. War seems to erupt naturally wherever human beings are found. War rivals sex as the primary force for the movement and distribution of people and resources on the planet. War is celebrated even in such sacred texts such as the Old Testament. For example, Joshua succeeded Moses and led the Israelites to conquer Canaan. Joshua conquered more than thirty kingdoms and killed their people and took their land—the "promised land." War, violence, and genocide are central activities of the Old Testament. Raymund Schwager[2], who is an Old Testament professor, points out a hundred passages in the Bible where God expressly commands others to kill people, and several stories where God is about to kill for no apparent reason (e.g., Exodus 4:24–26).

Now let me give you a little background. I am suspicious when you tell me that your God told you to kill me. I am suspicious when you tell me that your God tells you to come and take my land. And yet in the Bible, in the Old Testament, the Israelites say that God told them to take the promised land and kill all the people there. I am suspicious because claiming direction from God was the same justification used to kill Native Americans in this country. This was the new promised land, and the Europeans were the new Israelites.

The New Testament, however, is centered in the resurrection of Jesus Christ, and Jesus inaugurates the kingdom of God, a new order of human behavior that does not use violence to resolve human conflict and does not project human violence onto God. We have to be careful, because if you say that your God told you to kill me, how do you know that you are not projecting your human violence onto God? But despite the inauguration of the kingdom of God, the consummation of the kingdom will only occur after the final war between good and evil and God and Satan as foretold in Revelation 20. After reading Revelation 20, I am even more convinced with Einstein that "as long as there is man there will be war."

But despite the universality and the seeming permanency of war, we have a hard time agreeing on a definition of it. War has been called everything from a "great adventure" to "hell on earth." Prussian military genius Carl von Clausewitz insisted that "War is merely the continuation of policy by another means."[3] When we can't get it done by negotiation, we continue the same policy by another means. In contrast, a popular song of the 1970s rhetorically asked and answered the question of war: "War! What is it good for? Absolutely nothing!" Is war a great adventure? Or is war hell on earth? Is war a continuation of policy by another means? Or is war good for absolutely nothing?

It is important to define war. War is conflict between social groups that is resolved by individuals on one or both sides killing those on the opposite side. The ethical dimensions of war can be defined by but cannot be limited to four modes of thought.

1. *The unjust or the offensive war:* This type of war is characterized by the intention of a group to steal what another group owns and leave them dead.

2. *The war of self-defense:* This type of war demonstrates the effort and the intent to prevent others from stealing from and killing one's group.

3. *The tradition of pacifism and nonviolence:* A chief proponent of this tradition, Dr. Martin Luther King, Jr., taught that war is idiocy. War will cause humanity to go into a spiral staircase spinning down into nuclear disintegration. You will shoot me, and I will shoot you; you will shoot me with a bigger gun, and I will shoot you with a bigger gun, and together we will go down and down and down until finally, some fool will press a button, and nuclear winter will be visited upon the earth. That's the idiocy of war, according to Dr. Martin Luther King. "The choice is not between violence and nonviolence, but between nonviolence and nonexistence," he said.[4] We don't hear this quote of Dr. King's much. Instead, we hear "I have a dream." But King said that the choice is not violence or nonviolence, but nonviolence or nonexistence.

4. *The holy war or the crusade:* In the holy war, we invoke the name of God to totally exterminate the "infidels" or the "nonbelievers." Christians can only be half jaundiced at Osama bin Laden, for if we read our Christian history, we

will see that we have carried on some crusades and pogroms too. Christians slaughtered some Jewish people in the name of Jesus because "some Jews had Christ put to death." In the name of God, we Christians have killed millions of people. The majority of the American public and many nations of the world define the September 11 attack as an act of offensive war and provocation. Our response is a just war of self-defense. America is at war, as President Bush says, "to protect freedom, democracy, and our way of life."

My concern is that evil tends to mask itself in the cloak of war. Some of the most gruesome, inhumane, and despicable acts known to humankind have been perpetrated under the guise of a just war, and often in the name of God. Can we truly distinguish war from the evil that so often disguises itself in the clothing of war? Or is war inherently evil so that every time we go to war, we are engaging in an evil act? Or must we go to war to stop the march of evil? As I think about September 11, and our response of war, the words of Jesus in Matthew 6:13—in the midst of what is commonly called the Lord's Prayer—ring loudly in my soul: "Deliver us from evil."

Jesus understood the true power, nature, size, scope, depth, reality, and impact of evil. Jesus understood that evil is so despicable, so desperate, so depraved, so destructive, so vicious, and so able to bring misery and pain that he simply prayed that we would be delivered from it. Jesus understood that evil fundamentally does not make sense. How does one make sense of evil? What are the rhyme and the reason, the rationale and the thinking of evil? What sense does evil make? Jesus knew better than anybody that evil has never made sense and never will make sense.

Evil is our tearing up for the hell of it, our killing people for the hell of it, our destroying the fabric of lives, families, and nations for the sheer hell of it. No purpose. Just for the hell of it! No end in mind. Just for the hell of it! No justification. Just for the hell of it! Evil runs airplanes into buildings, but evil can also bomb an already decimated country. Evil has many faces; terrorism might be one and patriotism another. Evil can lurk not only in the Taliban and Osama bin Laden, but also in President Bush and the U.S. Congress. Evil can show up in any country, at any time, strike in any party or any government. Evil can be personal evil—a child is raped or abused. Evil can be structural—an entire people are given "Bantu" education that limits, if not cuts off, their futures. Evil can locate itself in individual people such as Hitler, and also in entire societies—in the courts, in the police force, in the banks, in the schools, and even in the churches, which sanctioned the slave trade, apartheid, Jim Crow, and the genocide of Rwandans. Evil has so many faces that evil essentially is faceless.

Jesus was so aware of the devastating power of evil that he prayed that we would be delivered from it. "Deliver us from evil."

Jesus' prayer recognizes several painful realities that we must come to terms with and that are contained within the lessons of the attack on September 11. First, we must ask God to deliver us from evil because human resources are inadequate to deal with evil and all its eventualities, possibilities, and circumstances, however well planned and organized the human resources may be. In other words, we should prepare security checkpoints; we should gather intelligence; we should screen luggage and do absolutely everything at our human disposal to protect our safety, but we must recognize that our human resources cannot prepare for every eventuality. I don't care how many security personnel screen luggage or how many National Guard troops patrol airports with rifles. They ought to be there, but we still cannot prepare for every possibility or every eventuality. Life has a certain fragility. So when Jesus says, "Deliver us from evil," he means there is a certain amount of weakness and destructiveness that is a permanent part of the world that can only be defined as evil. It is in the fabric and structure of things. So why should I stop flying? I can stop flying and be run over on my way out of church. When we connect Jesus' "Deliver us from evil" to September 11, it raises the concern that no matter how well organized we are, life still has a certain fragility.

This leads to a second painful reality that we must come to terms with. Jesus prayed "Deliver us from evil," realizing that not everybody is going be delivered. In this sphere of human existence, not all of us are going to be delivered from evil. Some people died in the collapsing structure and debris of the World Trade Center. Some die when people with bombs strapped onto themselves walk into shopping centers and explode themselves along with their victims' lives, hopes, and dreams. Some die from state-sponsored terrorism, ethnic cleansing, and genocide. Whole nations of Native American people died as America waged an offensive holy war for this land. Some children are molested, and some people are raped. Some innocent folk do die at the hands of drive-by shooters and would-be robbers. Martin Luther King, Jr., lay dead on the balcony of the Lorraine Motel in Memphis from an assassin's bullet. Not all of us will escape the tentacles and the clutches of evil. It is not possible for all of us to be delivered from its desperate and despicable acts. Life is fragile, and fragility could happen to you. Evil could happen to you. That's why you ought to kiss somebody today. That's why you ought to say a kind word to somebody today. That's why you ought to stop playing church today. That's why you ought to love somebody today. Life is fragile.

If we are not careful, these painful realities will lead us to a fear of the future. When Jesus prayed "Deliver us from evil," he meant that we could not get around the fact that the future is uncertain; therefore, living becomes an act of faith, not just an act of planning. This does not mean that we ought not plan. It does mean, however, that living is not an act of planning. It is an act of faith! Living is not an act of control.

It is an act of trust. This does not mean that we should not have goals, directions, and plans, but we must understand that we are not in as much control as we think.

This kind of prayerful living is further complicated by the fact that we must not only be concerned with being victims of evil, we must also watch the ways that we can so easily further the destructive and uncreative aims of evil. If we are not careful, we will easily cooperate with evil. We will actively perpetrate evil, and our silence and our acquiescence will allow evil to flourish. Our patriotism, our nationalism, our military, our economic superiority, and our technology can be instruments of evil. President Bush and his cabinet have such great power at their fingertips, so we must pray for them. I ask God to deliver Mr. Bush and his cabinet from evil because they have such great means of destruction at their disposal. For instance, there are heat-seeking sensors in the sky that can target a bomb to hit a cave by detecting the presence of body heat in the cave in the dead of winter. That's power. Without a doubt, we have military superiority and economic superiority, but we don't want to use them to perpetrate evil. That's also what Jesus meant when he said, "Deliver us from evil." Deliver us from perpetrating evil. Deliver us from being silent in the face of evil. Deliver us from taking the easy way out by acquiescing with evil. Not only do we want evil to not be perpetrated on us, we don't want to perpetrate evil on others.

Now I know this message sounds gloomy, yet there is a word of hope. Jesus would not teach us to ask for deliverance if deliverance were not available. Deliverance is available. Evil can do its worst, but deliverance is still available. Thousands can fall at the World Trade Center, but evil will not have the last word. No matter what evil does, evil will not win. Evil will not have the last word. Jesus suffered crucifixion at the hands of evil. Jesus died under the hand of evil. Jesus was buried in a borrowed tomb at the hands of evil. But the resurrection is the guarantor that evil will not win, that death will not have the victory. The resurrection is the guarantee that we will not be overcome.

Planes will run into buildings and thousands will die, but we will not be overcome. Wars can ravage the landscape of our world, but we will not be overcome. We might be raped and molested, but we will not be overcome. We may have had "Bantu" education and had our families killed because they were Tutsis, but we will not be overcome. A poet said, "The wheels of justice grind slowly, but they grind exceedingly fine." A poet said, "A lie cannot live forever, and truth that is crushed to the earth will rise again." We shall not be overcome. The Bible says in Galatians 6:7 that God is not mocked, that you shall reap what you sow. We shall not be overcome. The Bible says, "Don't fret yourself because of evildoers, for soon they shall be cut off" (paraphrase of Ps. 37:1, 9). We will not be overcome. We can take courage that right defeated is more powerful than evil triumphant. Jesus gives us the assurance that evil will not have the last word because evil did not have the last word with him.

Julian of Norwich (c.1342–1416), the great English mystic, says in *The Revelation of Divine Love,* "We are given comfort in these matters of all tribulation. Because he said not, 'Thou shalt not be troubled. Thou shalt not be travailed. Thou shalt not be distressed.' He said, 'Thou shalt not be overcome.'" That's what he said. In other words, you cannot get out of here without trials and tribulation and troubles and distress. But the promise is, "Thou shalt not be overcome." He doesn't say you won't have heartbreak. He doesn't say that death might not find your address. He does not say that you might not be shot and killed. He does not say that evil will not come to your address. But he says, "Thou shalt not be overcome." I think Jesus said it this way: "In this world, you will have tribulation, but be of good cheer; I have overcome the world."

Notes

[1] *Time* 154, no. 27 (31 December 1999).

[2] Raymund Schwager, *Must There Be Scapegoats? Violence and Redemption in the Bible* (San Francisco: Harper & Row, 1987), 46–67, 119.

[3] Michael P. Ghiglieri, *The Dark Side of Man: Tracing the Origins of Male Violence* (Reading, Mass.: Perseus Books, 1999), 160.

[4] Quoted in James Washington, ed., *A Testament of Hope: The Essential Writings of Martin Luther King, Jr.* (San Francisco: Harper & Row, 1986), 276.

Faith in the End of the Story

"For thine is the kingdom, and the power, and the glory"

Usually I would ask you to take your Bibles and turn to our text for today. I cannot do that today because our text is not found in some of the Bibles that you are holding. The text of the Lord's Prayer in the New Testament does not end with "Thine is the kingdom, and the power, and the glory forever, Amen." Matthew ends with "lead us not into temptation," and immediately goes to a short exhortation on forgiveness. Luke ends with deliver us from evil, and immediately goes on teaching about persistence in prayer. So how do we get this doxology—"For thine is the kingdom, and the power, and the glory"?

The simple and plain truth is that the church added it. In the fourth century, the church added, "Thine is the kingdom, power, and glory" to the text. It was added to the gospel of Matthew and was carried until modern biblical scholars concurred that it was a late addition to the text, and some translations left it out. Most of us have heard it all our lives and are therefore shocked to discover that it is actually a late addition into the text. Why did the fourth-century church feel the need to add this doxology?

I believe it is there because we could not be left with the reality of evil and the severity of temptation. The church in its understanding of the prayer and sensitivity to life realized that "deliver us from evil" and "lead us not into temptation" are too perilous a note to end the prayer, though that is where Jesus ended it. Again, Jesus understood the true reality and nature of evil. Jesus understood that evil was so vicious and destructive that he prayed that we would be delivered from evil. And it is something unsettling to be left with the reality of evil as the last word. The last word out of Jesus' mouth was that evil is so terrible that I am going to pray that you be delivered from it and that you not be led into temptation. The church could grasp the true and present danger in the reality of evil. The church made the decision to end the prayer in positive affirmation. The church said even if we have to go through evil, "thine is the kingdom, and the power, and the glory." We might have to go through evil, but we can be delivered from it because "thine is the kingdom, and the power, and the glory."

What does this doxology mean? Thine is the kingdom, and the power, and the glory is the affirmation of faith that we will prevail in the end, despite the most brutal and honest facts and assessments of our current reality. No matter how evil evil is, God alone is the kingdom, power, and glory. This last statement is not mine, and so let me tell you this story.[1]

Admiral Jim Stockdale was the highest-ranking U.S. military officer in the Hanoi prison camp during the Vietnam War. He was imprisoned for eight years, tortured many times, and lived without any prisoner's rights, no set release date, and no certainty as to whether he would ever again see his family. He fought an internal war against his captors and their attempts to use the prisoners for propaganda. At one point, he beat himself with a stool and cut himself with a razor, deliberately disfiguring himself so that he could not be put on video as an example of "well-treated" prisoners. Knowing that discovery would mean torture and perhaps death, he exchanged secret intelligence information with his wife through their letters. After his release, he was given the highest military and civilian awards and commendation.

When interviewed he said, "I never lost faith in the end of the story. I never doubted not only that I would get out, but also that I would prevail in the end and turn the experience into the defining event of my life, that, in retrospect, I would not trade." The interviewer asked him—who did not make it out? "The optimists. They were the ones who said, 'We're going to be out by Christmas.' And Christmas would come and Christmas would go. Then they'd say, 'We're going to be out by Easter.' And Easter would come and Easter would go. And then Thanksgiving, and then it would Christmas again, and they would die of a broken heart."

In summing it all up he said,

> This is a very important lesson. You must never confuse faith that you will prevail in the end—which you can never afford to lose—with the need for discipline to confront the most brutal facts of your current reality, whatever they might be.

This is the affirmation of thine is the kingdom, and the power, and the glory—it is the faith that we will prevail in the end. God and God alone is the kingdom, the power, and the glory. No matter what happens, God is the kingdom and the power and the glory. And because God is the kingdom and the power and the glory, because you belong to God, you can prevail in the end. This is important because you can never afford to lose the belief that you will prevail in the end. If you give that up, if you lose that, then you have been swallowed up in temptation and trial. You have fallen into the hands of the evil one.

Do not be optimists. Do not assume that what you are going through will be over by Christmas—then when Christmas passes, you say Easter—then when Easter passes, you say Thanksgiving—then you get to Christmas again and die of a broken heart. I do not know how long you are going to have to go through what you are going through. I do not know how long the storm will last. I do not know how dark the night will get. You are in something that could be the defining moment of your life, and it is going to take time. Get yourself set for a long duration. Bunker down and trench because the way is hard, the road is rough, and the hills are hard to climb. But do not give up the belief that you will prevail in the end. Do not give up! Do not quit. For we know someone who is the kingdom and the power and the glory.

Notice what Stockdale says—you must combine faith in the fact that you will prevail with the discipline to confront the most brutal facts of your current reality, whatever they might be. What are the most brutal facts of your present reality—you are lonely; you are tired; you have cancer; your health is fading; your children will not obey you; you have made some mistakes, some bad choices; you are living in the land of mistakes and regret, thinking of what you would do if you had the chance to do it over again? What are the most brutal facts of our current reality? Thirty-five hundred dying in the World Trade Center bombing?

It makes no difference what the brutal facts say; this will be the defining moment of my life. Not only shall I prevail but this will be the defining event of my life that, in retrospect, I would not trade. I will have the victory. This thing that I am going through is going to bless me. This pain that I am shouldering will be a defining moment of my life.

Several years ago, I was in Capetown, South Africa. It was during the second of the three championship runs of Michael Jordan and the Chicago Bulls. The Bulls were up three to two on somebody in the best-of-seven series and were trying to close the opponents out. In Africa, they did not show the game live, but on tape delay at three o'clock in the morning. By the time that I watched it, the game was already over. I could have turned over to CNN and found out who won the game before watching it, but that would have killed the suspense, and so I watched not knowing the score. The Bulls were losing in the first quarter, but not to worry because we had been down in the first quarter before. We were losing in the second quarter, but not to worry because it was still early. We were losing in the third quarter, and I became a bit concerned. But along about the fourth quarter things got really tough. I think the Bulls were down thirteen points with five minutes to go. All of a sudden I started to bite my nails, and it got real tense. My anxiety got so high that it dawned on me that I could just turn over the channel and find out who won the game. I got so nervous and upset about the outcome that I turned over to CNN and found out who won the game. CNN was functioning in real time, while the game was on tape delay. The battle had already been fought and the victory had already been won. I found out that the Bulls had won, and then I went back to the other channel to watch the rest of it. It was easier to watch because I knew the end of the story. It was easier to watch the score because even though we were trailing in the tape delay time zone, we had already won in real time.

That is what the church did when it added "For thine is the kingdom, and the power, and the glory." It switched you over to another time. The church took you from tape delay to real time—from an earthly perspective to a heavenly view. While you are nervous and upset with evil, while you are distressed and distraught, the church says to change the channel. "Thine is the kingdom, and the power, and the glory." God is greater and stronger and more powerful than evil. All things are in God's hands. The battle has already been fought, and the victory has already been won. God will take care of and redeem all evil. God is the kingdom, God is the power, and God is the glory. Never lose faith in the end of the story.

Note

[1]Story and quotes from Jim Collins, "In Recession, Face Brutal Facts, Thrive," *USA Today,* 27 November 2001, 15A.

The God of the Amen[1]

"Amen!"

Edward Hooper points out in his landmark work *The River: A Journey to the Source of HIV and AIDS*[2] that pathological liars are rare. Most people are honest if only because that is the easiest way to live with the most self-respect and a minimum of complications. However, for most people there does seem to be a sliding scale—a point at which lying becomes an option. Many will lie when their self-image is threatened, or their financial future is at stake, or to protect their family or friends. Only a few people have the integrity to tell the truth regardless of the circumstances or the consequences. Most of us have integrity on some form of sliding scale.

Hooper goes on to say that the process of lying is interesting. One starts by swerving around the sharper and more dangerous corners of what is known to be true to arrive at a position that is almost true. This allows one to maintain two parallel versions of the truth: one for the heart, or perhaps for the best friend or for the spouse in the dead of night, and the other less precise version for the potential enemy, for the person who asks awkward questions, and for those who might do one harm. Time passes. Recollections become less sharp. The two parallel versions of truth fade in and out and intertwine. Finally, the process is completed. Two apples become three apples; a chimp changes to a giraffe; a zebra to a crocodile; and the truth becomes a lie. And as far as one remembers, one was not even there at the time in question. Sometimes only God knows what the truth is.

But what if one learned to live in truth and believed that truth was truth and that truth is the same for the friend as for the enemy? What if one did not have parallel versions, but one truth? This is the essence and the nature of God: the complete, unswerving, and absolute truth. God cannot lie. God cannot evade the truth. God is the God of truth. With God, two apples cannot become three apples, a chimp cannot change to a giraffe, nor a zebra to a crocodile. With God, the truth cannot become a lie. God does not swerve around the sharper edges of what is known to arrive at something almost true. God is faithful, and God's testimonies and precepts are sure. God is the complete, unswerving, and absolute truth.

And when we hear the complete, unswerving, and absolute truth, all we can say is Amen. To every word that proceeds out of the mouth of God you can say Amen. For anything truthful you say about God, you can say Amen. Whenever God's name is mentioned, you can say Amen. Any time you mention one of God's attributes, you must say Amen. The biblical editors addressed evil and said, "Thine is the kingdom, and the power, and the glory." And when they talked about God being the kingdom, the power, and the glory, it was so absolutely true that they had to add, "Amen." There cannot be a doxology—a brief praise speech unto God—without an Amen. Whenever we talk about God, somebody ought to say Amen. God is the God of Amen. When we hear the complete, unswerving, and absolute truth, all we can say is Amen.

Amen is an adjective that literally means firm, true, sound, and reliable. The speaker, to express confidence, assurance, and dependability in the truth that has been expressed, says Amen. It means, "It shall be so" and "So let it be." To say Amen is to say, "I tell you that it is true." To say Amen is to say, "So we believe it is." To say Amen is to say, "It is done."

Amen means truly, truly. Amen means surely, surely. Amen means sho'nuff, sho'nuff. The Lord Jesus said Amen, translated "verily, verily," to introduce new revelations of the mind of God. "Verily, verily, I say unto thee," except you be born again, you cannot see the kingdom of God (paraphrase of John 3:3). All God's promises are "yes" and "amen" in Christ (2 Cor. 1:20). All God's promises are firm, reliable, and sure in Christ Jesus; all God's promises are complete, unswerving, and absolutely true in Christ Jesus. God's promises are so real that Amen is the title of Christ in Revelation 3:14. "To the angel of the church in Laodicea write: These are the words of the Amen, the faithful and true witness, the ruler of God's creation." God is the God of Amen, the God of absolute truth, and the God who is firm, true, and sure.

But how can we say Amen when we are living with parallel versions of the truth? How can we say Amen when we are not living Amen, when we are not living the truth? Religious people kill others in the name of God and then say Amen. Osama bin Laden kills in the name of God and then says Amen. Christians contradict the truth of God with their behavior and then say Amen. Swerving and avoiding the sharper and more dangerous corners of what is true about God, Christians come up with parallel versions of truth and double standards of behavior, one for the friend and one for the enemy. Christians change a zebra into a crocodile, an elephant into a mouse, and a lie into the truth. Too often churches in America are about swerving and avoiding the sharper and more dangerous corners of what is true. Churches are made up of the majority of us who have a hard time facing the truth. We will say that God is truth, and we will say Amen, but when we have to live the truth and live our Amen, many of us fall short.

We are this way because truth is often painful. Gardner Taylor says, "Truth is ultimately kind, but often initially painful." But I want to help you today by letting you know that though truth is painful, there are two kinds of pain. According to David Schnarch, there is a difference between "clean pain" and "dirty pain."[3] Dirty pain is the pain that comes when one refuses to accept the truth. It is the pain of self-denial, the pain of self-avoidance, the pain of refusing to tell the truth to yourself about yourself. It is the pain of defending, denying, or deflecting to keep from seeing or doing something difficult. Dirty pain is the pain of repeated mistakes promoted through self-imposed blindness. Schnarch says, "the dirty feeling comes from dodging yourself." People experience *clean pain* when they finally accept an accurate self-picture, when they finally accept the truth regardless of what it does to their self-image or self-concept. The truth is the truth. If I am a liar, I am a liar. If I have not done as I ought to have done, then I have not done as I ought to have done. Clean pain has to do with moving forward from an accurate self-picture, accepting what has been, is, and will be. Clean pain is about self-acceptance of who one really is or what one has really done.

The problem is that it is hard to accept myself for who I really am and what I have really done without God. But I can accept the truth about myself because I know there is a God of truth who will take me right where I am, a God of truth who will say, "Now that you are ready to deal with the truth, I am the truth, and so you are now ready to deal with me. And if you deal with me in truth, then I can work with you. I am the Way, the Truth, and the Life. I am faithful and sure." When we come to the point that we are ready to deal with truth about ourselves, we have help available from the One who is the truth. God says, "I do not care what the truth is about you. I do not care if you are drug addicted, sexually addicted, alcohol addicted, or any kind of other addicted. I do not care if you are a pimp, liar, adulterer, sinner, broken, depressed, sick and diseased, suffering from low self-esteem, raped, misused, abused, rich, poor, misinformed, miseducated, misunderstood, or otherwise. I am the truth, and let me tell you three things about my truth:

First, my truth, my word of revelation, is beyond any human imagination.

I see you in my divine imagination, and in my word of revelation, I reveal the things I see concerning you. I see you beyond yourself. I see you already healed. I see you beyond the capacity of your human imagination. I see where you are headed. I see what you can become. I formed you in your mother's womb and knew you before you were known to the world. I will reveal my plan for you, and you will discover that it is beyond any human imagination. I do not care where you are now; I created you and will reveal to you your end in my divine imagination.

Second, my truth, my word of command, is the absolute unveiling of human duty and human perfection.

Because I know you in my divine imagination, I see you already perfected, and through my word of command I will reveal to you your human duty. I will issue my word of command and reveal to you how you should act and how you should behave. I will reveal to you what you are responsible for and who you are accountable to. I will show you the ethics and standards of someone who is true, who is my follower in truth. I will reveal to you what you were created to do. I brought you forth to do your human duty in human perfection, and my word of command is the absolute unveiling of my plan.

Third, my truth, my word of promise, is that on which you can rest all of your weight and be safe forever.

If you walk in divine imagination and follow my unveiled plan for human duty, and if you move in the sphere of my human perfection, then you can rest and be safe forever. There is nothing in the world that you can put your full weight on.

My promise is the only thing that will hold your weight. On my word of promise you can go to sleep and know that I neither sleep nor slumber. On my word of promise you can go to work knowing that the One who keepeth the stars in the sky and worlds from colliding together keepeth thee. You can go through the fire and not get burned. You can walk in the storm and never lose your way. You can tread with snakes and not die from a bite. I am the God of truth. I am the God of the Amen. You live by my word of revelation of the divine imagination; you live by my word of command that unveils human duty and human perfection; you live by my word of promise that will keep you safe forever.

> *My word is absolutely reliable.*
> *My word is absolutely dependable.*
> *My word is absolutely unfailing.*
> *My word is absolutely trustworthy.*
> *My word is absolutely responsible.*
> *My word is absolutely solid.*
> *My word is absolutely sound.*
> *My word is absolutely true.*
> *I am the God of the Amen.*

When humans speak, they must back up their speech with quotes and verification by certain experts, sources, and authorities; but when I speak, I am my own backup. I am my own authority. I have the right and the authority to lay my utterances down before you and expect you to take them for no other reason than [that] I said it. I am the God of the Amen."

And in response to hearing the complete, unswerving, and absolute truth, all we can say is Amen. When humans speak, our response is "perhaps." When humans speak, our response is "maybe." When humans speak, our response is "I suppose." When humans speak, our word is "I hope so." But when God speaks, the human word is Amen. God is the God of Amen.

In response to hearing the complete, unswerving, and absolute truth, all we can say is Amen.

The writer of Romans, after hearing the complete, unswerving, and absolute truth for sixteen chapters, says at the end, "To the only wise God be glory forever through Jesus Christ! Amen" (Rom. 16:27). At the end of First Corinthians, the writer, after hearing the complete, unswerving, and absolute truth, says: "My love to all of you in Christ Jesus. Amen" (1 Cor. 16:24). At the end of Second Corinthians in response to the absolute truth: "The grace of the Lord Jesus Christ, and the love of God, and the communion of the Holy Ghost, be with you all. Amen" (2 Cor. 13:14, KJV). At the end of Galatians: "The grace of our Lord Jesus Christ be with your spirit. Amen" (Gal. 6:18, KJV). At the end of Ephesians: "Grace be with all them who love our Lord Jesus Christ in sincerity. Amen" (Eph. 6:24, KJV). At the end of Philippians: "The grace of our Lord Jesus Christ be with you all. Amen" (Phil. 4:23, KJV). At the end of 1 Thessalonians: "The grace of our Lord Jesus Christ be with you. Amen" (1 Thess. 5:28, KJV). At the end of Jude: "To the only wise God our Saviour, be glory and majesty, dominion and power, both now and ever. Amen" (Jude 25, KJV).

Likewise, in the book of Revelation, the writer, after hearing the complete, unswerving, and absolute truth, must say Amen: "And hath made us kings and priests unto God and his Father, to him be glory and dominion for ever and ever. Amen" (Rev. 1:6, KJV). "Behold he cometh with the clouds; and every eye shall see him, and they also which pierced him: and all kindreds of the earth shall wail because of him. Even so, Amen" (Rev. 1:7, KJV). "And all the angels stood round about the throne, and about the elders and the four beasts, and fell before the throne on their faces, and worshipped God, saying, Amen: Blessing, and glory, and wisdom, and thanksgiving, and honor, and power, and might, be unto our God for ever and ever. Amen" (Rev. 7:11–12, KJV). "And the four and twenty elders and the four beasts fell down and worshipped God that sat on the throne, saying, Amen" (Rev. 19:4, KJV). "He which testifieth these things saith, Surely I come quickly. Amen. Even so, come, Lord Jesus. The grace of our Lord Jesus Christ be with you all. Amen" (Rev. 22:20–21, KJV).

In response to hearing the complete, unswerving, and absolute truth, all we can say is Amen. The editor wrote, "Thine is the kingdom, and the power, and the glory." It was so much the complete, unswerving, and absolute truth that all the writer could say was, "Amen."

Notes

[1]Title is borrowed from Caesar Clark, *The God of the Amen,* The African American Pulpit, vol. 3, no. 3, Summer 2000 (Valley Forge, Pa.: Judson Press), 9.

[2]Edward Hooper, *The River: A Journey to the Source of HIV and AIDS* (Boston: Back Bay Books, 2000), 795.

[3]David Schnarch, *Passionate Marriage: Love, Sex, and Intimacy in Emotionally Committed Relationships* (New York: W.W. Norton, 1997), 352.